# DEERING LIBRARY

## AN ILLUSTRATED HISTORY

EDITOR
Nina Barrett

WRITERS
Russell Clement
Jeffrey Garrett
Janet Olson

PRIMARY PHOTOGRAPHER
Peter Kiar

PHOTO RESEARCHER
Allen Streicker

DESIGNER
Kim Bartko

The publication of this book was made possible by Stephen M. Strachan and Linda Denmark Strachan, and their children Kammer D. Strachan and Deaunne L. Denmark, in loving memory of Kammer's great-great-grandfather Charles Deering.

# DEERING LIBRARY

## AN ILLUSTRATED HISTORY

NORTHWESTERN UNIVERSITY LIBRARY

EVANSTON, ILLINOIS

Printed in the United States of America

10  9  8  7  6  5  4  3  2  1

ISBN-13: 978-0-8101-2502-5
ISBN-10: 0-8101-2502-1

Library of Congress Cataloging-in-Publication data are available from the Library of Congress.

♾ The paper used in this publication meets the minimum requirements of the American National Standard for Information Sciences—Permanence of Paper for Printed Library Materials, ANSI Z39.48-1992.

# CONTENTS

# ACKNOWLEDGMENTS

This book, like Deering Library itself, could not have been created without the enthusiastic support and invaluable expertise of the library's staff and friends. Specifically, though in no particular order, the authors would like to gratefully acknowledge:

Northwestern University Archives, which holds the official documents and publications that supplied background and context about Northwestern history and the design, construction, and use of Deering Library. Also in the Archives are the personal papers, biographical files, student newspapers, and ephemera that revealed the life of the building over time. The thousands of historic images in the Archives' photographic files could have filled multiple volumes—this book contains a mere sampling. The resources of the Archives are the result of university archivist Patrick M. Quinn's thirty-four years of collecting and preserving materials relating to every aspect of the university's history. For their invaluable assistance with suggesting sources and correcting flights of fancy, Patrick Quinn and Kevin Leonard can add this book to a lengthy list of publications in which they are sincerely thanked. Allen Streicker chose and scanned the photographs used. Archives student employee Julie Fountain helped out on several important tasks.

While staff members throughout the library graciously supplied information and (most important) personal memories, everyone in the McCormick Library of Special Collections—Scott Krafft, Susan Lewis, and Sigrid Perry—went above and beyond, by digging for details, images, and reminiscences and by reading portions of the text. The Art Collection's Lindsay King provided editorial assistance, especially with the sections on James Gamble Rogers and Collegiate Gothic architecture.

The support and encouragement of the library's administration—especially Sarah Pritchard—and its board of governors was critical all along. Clare Roccaforte in the library's office of public relations helped the project off the launch pad and often made sure in the hectic months that followed that it stayed aloft. Alex Hernandez-Herrera, in the library's development office, was also a stalwart champion of the book. Claire Stewart, of Digital Collections, lent her expertise in copyright practices to the complex task of tracing and obtaining photo permissions. And the staff at Northwestern University Press—especially Donna Shear, Anne Gendler, and A. C. Racette—skillfully translated the vision of the book that was in the authors' heads into the culmination of that vision, which you hold in your hands.

The book is also a product of the artistry of two other contributors: Peter Kiar, who photographed Deering Library with a patience and a passion that exquisitely illuminate its beauty, and Kim Bartko, whose design work makes both words and pictures spring to life on these pages.

We gratefully acknowledge the R. R. Donnelley Foundation for its support of programming related to Deering Library's seventy-fifth anniversary.

Finally, the authors deeply appreciate the concern and generosity that members of the Deering and McCormick families have shown to Northwestern University Library over the course of several generations. In particular, a gift from Stephen and Linda Strachan ensured that this book could be as wonderful as the authors hoped it would be.

# GREETING

Henry S. Bienen
*President,*
*Northwestern University*

great library is at the heart of a great university. Thus, one of the first things I did on being appointed the fifteenth president of Northwestern University was to visit the library. I did this even before my official arrival in January 1995. I had visited the Africana collection when I was a graduate student at the University of Chicago, since it was and is the best in the world. Over my years as president, I came to visit the library often and to consider it as a portal for information flowing into Northwestern; a storage house; and a place where we disseminate knowledge.

Deering Library was designed to be the symbolic heart of Northwestern University, looking both backward toward the great intellectual traditions of the past and forward to the role Northwestern scholars would play in the world's future. James Gamble Rogers's Collegiate Gothic design for the building was meant to evoke Oxford and Cambridge, and the long European tradition in which Western education had its roots. But inside, the building was designed to provide state-of-the-art functionality for the librarians and the scholars who worked there every day. A British librarian who visited in 1933, the year Deering opened, marveled that it combined "the beauty of age with absolute newness and every modern equipment," especially "an ingenious contrivance for obtaining books from other departments" (essentially, a dumbwaiter).

In the seventy-five ensuing years, the future, we might say, has arrived, and to some extent has engulfed Rogers's small architectural gem. Especially with the construction of the Lakefill, the boundaries of the Evanston campus expanded, placing

Deering even more squarely at its heart. The three towers of the new Main Library, opened in 1970, emphasized the antiquity of Deering's design while also usurping its status as a state-of-the-art library; this newcomer was the library that would see us into the electronic age. Yet that development, too, enhanced Deering's identity as our symbolic heart. Now the repository for many of our most famous and treasured collections—our world-renowned Music Library, our impressively diverse McCormick Library of Special Collections, and the University Archives that serve as Northwestern's institutional memory—it houses many of the materials that give our library its distinct identity among the great American research libraries.

Entering its fourth quarter-century, Deering still looks both forward and back, albeit from a slightly different vantage point. Built to resemble an intellectual heirloom, it has actually become an intellectual heirloom—one that we in the Northwestern family cherish deeply, tend carefully, and will take care to pass on to coming generations, along with all the history—so beautifully documented in *Deering Library: An Illustrated History*—that it embodies.

# FOREWORD

When the authors of this book began combing through Northwestern's amazingly rich archives for historical information on the library that's named for my great-great-grandfather Charles Deering, one of the photographs they found was this shot of my granduncle Roger S. McCormick laying the cornerstone of the library in 1932, when he was twelve years old. They also found the text of the entry he wrote in his diary that day about the ceremony, which began.

> Well, the big ordeal is over and it was not so bad after all. When Grandmother told me that I had been chosen to lay the cornerstone of the new library which bears Grandfather's name I thought I could not do it because I had no experience in laying cornerstones and I was afraid that as a mason I would be a flop. But Grandmother told me that it was an honor to be chosen to represent the family and that I should feel proud to help. One thing to be thankful for, I was excused from school all afternoon.

I was touched and charmed to discover Roger's thoughts on this solemn occasion, because I remember a similar event at the library in 1989, when I was about the same age. It was a ceremony to unveil a portrait of my grandfather, Charles Deering McCormick, who had established the library's Charles Deering McCormick Endowment in 1986, and introduce a bookplate commemorating my father, Hilleary McCormick, which was to be placed in every book acquired with endowment funds.

Like Roger McCormick in his fine tweed coat and cap, I was all dressed up for the occasion in a satin-trimmed dress, with a big satin bow in my hair. And

NANCY McCORMICK VELLA

Roger S. McCormick lays the cornerstone for the Charles Deering Library on January 12, 1932.

xi

Nancy McCormick Vella attends a Deering ceremony in the 1980s with her mother, Katherine McCormick, and her grandparents, Mr. and Mrs. Charles Deering McCormick.

like Roger, I was feeling pretty nervous and shy. There was a lot of hand-shaking and picture-taking with a lot of important-looking grown-ups. I was too young to understand exactly what all the fuss was about—though old enough to understand that having your portrait painted and hung in a place as impressive looking as Deering Library was an amazing honor.

I always knew that I was proud of my grandfather, and that the library was something he was passionate about supporting, and now as a grown-up, I understand why: because as Richard Frieder, then head of the Preservation Department, said in his speech dedicating my grandfather's portrait, it represents "the storehouse of knowledge upon which the university is based."

Deering Library is a tradition in my family—a tradition we grow up with that can seem intimidating before we are old enough to understand what it really represents. Now as an adult I also understand that Deering is a larger tradition—shared with generations of Northwestern students who studied in the intimate spaces of its cozy reading rooms and explored the wide-ranging, eclectic contents of its special collections. And also with a community of generous donors who, through their own contributions and endowments, continue to ensure that the spirit of learning the Charles Deering Memorial Library represents will be preserved, enlarged, and carefully tended for the generations that will come to share our tradition in future years.

# DEERING LIBRARY

## AN ILLUSTRATED HISTORY

The first Northwestern building was built in 1855 at the northwest corner of Davis and Hinman (where the Davis Street Fishmarket restaurant stands today) and was later moved to the lakeshore location pictured here. It contained classroom space, offices, the chapel, dormitory rooms—and the library.

FOWLER. Phot.

# WHISPERS BETWEEN BOOKS
## THE COLLECTIONS OF DEERING LIBRARY

*t sua fata habent libelli.* Books, too, have their fates. When the lights go dim at night in Deering Library, what stories do they tell each other, the books? Does the ninth-century vellum manuscript, richly inscribed in the careful Carolingian hand of a Reichenau monk, converse with the seventeenth-century printed book it envelops? Does the sixteenth-century catalog of the book fair in Frankfurt speak in hushed tones to its neighbors on a Deering bookshelf, sharing anecdotes of Frau Dürer's visits to Frankfurt, where she came from distant Nuremberg to sell her husband's works? Umberto Eco called the nocturnal coming-to-life of books on the shelves of a great library the *sussurri dei libri*: the "whispering of the books." If there be such whispers, then Deering Library must be wonderfully haunted.

The history of Deering Library is not just the story of its wondrous architecture, of the generations of students, famous scholars, and assiduous librarians who have spent their days and evenings and even lives there. It is also the story of the books and manuscripts and rare artifacts that have come to belong to its collections, often after centuries—even millennia, as in the case of Deering Library's cuneiform tablets—of passing through the hands of writers, publishers, booksellers, owners, and collectors.

What are these stories that the books tell? Taken together, they are the story of the collections of Deering Library. Some of these books and collections first resided in Northwestern's earlier library buildings—for example, the fledgling university's first home in the cramped quarters of Old College, although these were mainly the utili-

JEFFREY GARRETT
*Assistant University Librarian*
*for Special Libraries*

Northwestern's second library was a 1,400-square-foot room in University Hall.

Built in 1869, University Hall was designed by Gurdon P. Randall. The building, with its distinctive bell tower, has become a symbol of Northwestern University.

tarian collections of the college's founding years. Others—and indeed many others, some with fantastic stories behind them, as we shall see—originally came to rest in Northwestern's second library on the third floor of University Hall in the 1870s and '80s. Then there were the collections absorbed by Northwestern's first freestanding building devoted to books, the Orrington Lunt Library, occupied in 1894. Some of these collections which came to Deering Library have stayed there to this day and may stay there for centuries to come. Others, such as Northwestern's distinguished collection of Africana, were originally housed here, but were moved when the new Main Library building, designed by Walter Netsch, was completed in the early 1970s. But they are all Deering stories, and some of them should be told here.

There is, for example, the extraordinary tale of two cities—Berlin and Chicago—which brought one of Germany's most exquisite private libraries to the still-rugged American Northwest of 1870. Johannes Schulze (1786–1869), a high official in the Prussian educational bureaucracy and a friend and close associate of many German luminaries of the age—among them Goethe, Schopenhauer, Hegel, and Leopold von Ranke—had died in February 1869, leaving behind a library of over 20,000

The university's first purpose-built library, the Orrington Lunt Library, also housed the University Guild's art collection and meeting rooms for literary societies.

"My Covenant was with him of Life and Peace."

Orrington Lunt

Orrington Lunt (1815–1897), one of Northwestern's founders and a president of the board of trustees, contributed funds to build the Orrington Lunt Library.

Johannes Schulze, whose collection of 20,000 volumes was acquired by Northwestern University in 1870

volumes on shelves in his Berlin apartment. It was already a famous collection across the *Reich* of Otto von Bismarck. Library historian Georg Leyh described it in fact as one of the great private collections of the nineteenth century. In July 1869, Schulze's son Max offered his father's library to the Prussian government for the high but worthy price of 7,500 thaler—the equivalent of about U.S. $7,000 at the time. The Prussian government, with other things on its mind on the eve of war with France, declined the purchase. This turned out to be a golden opportunity for Northwestern. Daniel Bonbright, a Northwestern professor of Latin who had studied in Bonn and Göttingen, happened to be on a research visit in Paris at the time and heard from the American consul of the availability of Schulze's library. He immediately traveled to Berlin to inspect the collection, wisely also commissioning an independent evaluation by Wilhelm David Koner, the librarian at the Royal University in Berlin. Koner's report, dated March 17, 1870, extolled the value of this "painstakingly" assembled collection, concluding that

for a new university, where it is desired to establish a library in aid of the studies there to be pursued, the purchase of this collection remarkable in many directions, is to be warmly recommended. It would at least serve as an admirable nucleus around which a great library might gradually grow.

Following Bonbright's urgent recommendation, Northwestern's leadership acted quickly. University trustee Luther L. Greenleaf ceded ownership of two parcels of nearby land to cover the expense of purchase and shipping—as it turned out, just over a year before he would lose everything in the Great Chicago Fire. The "Greenleaf Library," as the purchase was named in his honor, increased the size of Northwestern's library sevenfold. With it, seventeen incunabula—the technical term for books printed during the fifteenth century, in the years immediately following Gutenberg's invention of the printing press—and dozens of richly produced volumes created by the famous printing dynasties of sixteenth- and seventeenth-century Europe came to the wooded shores of Lake Michigan. Among these were the earliest works printed in Greek by Aldus Manutius in Venice, scientific texts printed by Elsevir in the Netherlands in the 1600s and 1700s, and an entire library devoted to the life of Alexander the Great. As late as 1925, another German library

One of Northwestern's earliest faculty members, Daniel Bonbright (1831–1912) taught Latin, served as the librarian from 1858 to 1865, and was the interim president from 1900 to 1902.

historian, Karl M. Meyer, would express his "regret that this library could not have been kept for the Reich."

The Greenleaf Library is one of Northwestern's great treasures. Several thousand of its most valuable volumes reside today in Deering Library, including the ninth-century Carolingian manuscript mentioned at the outset of this chapter—which according to Northwestern history professor Robert Lerner may be the oldest medieval document held by any library in the Chicago area. Another of the most remarkable pieces to come into Deering Library as part of the Greenleaf Library was a volume of Johannes Schulze's own handwritten notes from Hegel's lectures on "The History of Philosophy" from the winter of 1820 to 1821 in Berlin, revised by Schulze in collaboration with Hegel himself. (It should not be forgotten that after Hegel's death in a cholera epidemic, Schulze would become the editor of Hegel's *Phenomenology of the Spirit*, in 1831.)

The books of Schulze's library surely whisper at night to one another in German, Latin, and ancient Greek.

About thirty years after the library of Johannes Schulze came to Northwestern, another story with a German connection began to unfold—and its traces are still to be found in the stacks of Deering Library. Walter Lichtenstein came to Northwestern as university librarian shortly after Lodilla Ambrose left in 1908. A respected bibliographer at Harvard, Lichtenstein had been the curator of the Hohenzollern Collection at Harvard College Library, created in honor of Kaiser Wilhelm's visit to Cambridge in 1902. At Northwestern, Lichtenstein worked hard and with success to catalog and classify hitherto "hidden" collections (roughly 40,000 volumes in his first few years alone), to increase the staff to acceptable levels, but above all, to expand the collections and to lobby for their adequate storage. Although he had no success with this latter goal—there would be no new library at Northwestern until the building of Deering Library was completed in 1933—Lichtenstein was smashingly successful with his work to enhance library collections. He conducted book-buying trips in Europe and, from 1913 to 1915, he also made several trips to South America, journeys that were in no small measure responsible for the growth of Northwestern's book collections from 75,000 to 116,000 during his ten-year tenure—not counting the growth of government publications from 50,000 to 85,000. Yet allegations of pro-German activities while he was in South America led to the confiscation of his passport and, in 1918, to his abrupt dismissal from Northwestern. Lichtenstein did not live out his days in ignominy, however. After being sacked by Northwestern, he began a successful career as a banker in Chicago and, in 1945, was called to Germany by the U.S. military government of Lucius Clay to serve as head of the Financial Institutions Division.

It is perhaps no exaggeration to say that Walter Lichtenstein's successes as a collection builder made the construction of a new library building inevitable—or at least created the pressing demand for such a building. Added to this were the increasingly voracious research and teaching needs of the Northwestern community. These are reflected in the huge increase in books coming in and out of the library: circulation more than doubled between 1908 and 1918, from 45,000 to 96,000. Space for collections and services was becoming desperately inadequate. Lichtenstein had placed the Latin and Greek collections into storage, yet window ledges, stairways, desks, and even user seating in Lunt Library were all gradually being converted into storage space. To grapple with these challenges (and to appoint a replacement for the dismissed Walter Lichtenstein), in 1919 the board of trustees appointed Theodore Wesley Koch (1871–1941) as the new university librarian. Koch presided over an exciting era in the history of the library, including the building of Deering Library. Koch's contributions ended only with his death.

Koch already had enjoyed a distinguished career as a librarian at such prestigious institutions as Cornell, the Library of Congress, and the University of Michigan. He was also a distinguished writer and *homme de lettres,* specializing—to the delight of Northwestern's faculty, students, and donor community—in bibliophile topics. For example, Koch translated Flaubert's *Bibliomanie* from the French (1929) and Julius R. Haarhaus's *Maculaturalia* from the German (1932), presenting these works at popular public meetings. But all the while he lobbied for a new building. Whether as a result of Koch's efforts or simply a fortuitous circumstance, the bequest to Northwestern by agricultural equipment magnate Charles Deering (1852–1927), announced in 1929, was earmarked for a new building. The result was Charles Deering Library, built in emulation of King's College Chapel, Cambridge. Opening in January 1933, with a capacity of five hundred thousand volumes (not including government publications) and seating for nine hundred readers, Deering Library finally offered adequate quarters for books and for users.

Bookplate pasted in each of the volumes from the Schulze collection

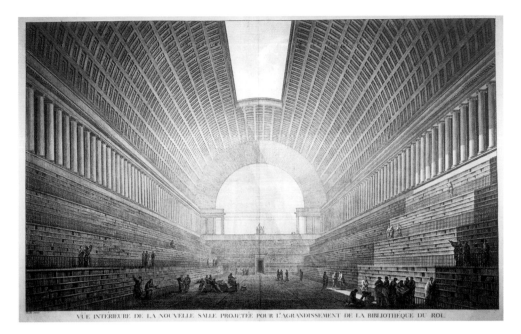

Engraving of the ideal library from Étienne-Louis Boullée, *Mémoire sur les moyens de procurer à la bibliothèque du roi...* (Paris, 1785)

Koch's reputation and charisma facilitated the gift of important books and collections to the university library—indeed, as earlier Northwestern University Library historian Rolf Erickson has pointed out, "it was not uncommon during his administration to find that the number of gift volumes often equaled that of volumes purchased." For example, Koch managed to attract a women's collection to Northwestern (now known as the Biblioteca Femina), a collection of 1,000 volumes assembled for the International Congress of Women, held in Chicago during the Century of Progress Exhibition in 1933, which has since expanded to include several thousand more. Koch also exploited the depressed book market of the 1930s to make buying trips. One example of a bibliographic treasure now in Deering Library is the extraordinary architectural portfolio of Étienne-Louis Boullée (1728–99), *Mémoire sur les moyens de procurer à la bibliothèque du roi les avantages que ce monument exige* (1785), purchased by Koch in London for a mere six pounds.

During his twenty-two-year tenure as university librarian, Koch presided over spectacular growth—trebling the collections from 120,000 to 377,000 volumes and increasing circulation, between 1931 and 1940, from 220,000 to 320,000. Upon his unexpected death in 1941, he was succeeded by valued assistant university librarian Effie A. Keith, who at the time of Koch's arrival had been head of catalog-

Reeve. Chaucer. Clerk of Oxenford. Cook. Miller. Wife of Bath. Merchant. Parson. Man of Law. Plowman. Physician. Franklin. 2 Citizens. Shipman. The Host. Sompnour. Manciple. Pardoner. Monk. Frier. a Citizen. Lady Abbess. Nun. 3 Priests. S

## CHAUCERS CANTERBURY PILGRIMS

*Painted in Fresco by William Blake & by him Engraved & Published October 8. 1810.* Ye gon to Canterbury God mote you spede.

Among the treasures housed in
Deering Library is this engraving
by poet and artist William Blake,
"Chaucers Canterbury Pilgrims,"
circa 1820.

ing and throughout her career enjoyed high standing as a competent administrator. Keith managed to make advances despite the war years. The two signal accomplishments of her administration were the creation of a 25,000-volume library for the new Technological Institute that opened in September 1942 and the acquisition of the library of anthropologist Franz Boas, numbering 15,000 volumes, through the efforts of new faculty member Melville J. Herskovits (1895–1963). This was the genesis of Northwestern's Africana library, now the single largest separate collection in the world of materials from or relating to Africa and known as the Melville J. Herskovits Library of African Studies.

Under Keith's successor, the Danish-born librarian Jens Nyholm (1900–83), the organizational contours of today's modern research library at Northwestern began to emerge. Earlier attempts under Lichtenstein and Koch to physically consolidate the various departmental libraries into a single, main library and to create a unified acquisitions budget had met some success, but foundered due to lack of space and then, after that issue had been resolved, on faculty resistance and lack of support for reorganization efforts by the university administration. Almost immediately upon arriving at Northwestern, Nyholm solicited and received the backing of university president Franklyn Snyder for either physically relocating departmental libraries to Deering or, at the very least, having them placed under the direction of the university librarian. In 1945, Nyholm assumed responsibility for the Technological Institute Library from the dean of the institute. Similar reorganization affected the Music and Curriculum libraries. Ultimately, the only remaining independent library on the Evanston campus was that of the Astronomy Department, which was not merged into the common administrative structure until 1961. With the exception of the Technological Institute Library, all of these libraries migrated to Deering Library.

As already observed, the history of Deering Library is also the history of its collections. With the completion of the new library building in the early 1970s and the move of Northwestern's "general" library collections away from Deering and into the new edifice, Deering Library began to become the university's special home for special libraries: the libraries whose books have the most stories to tell—and who are our library's most voluble whisperers at night.

This aerial view of the Evanston
campus in the 1920s, long before
the Lakefill project altered the
contours of the shoreline, shows
Fisk Hall at lower right, the Men's
Quads clustered toward the upper
left, and the Women's Quads under
construction at the lower left.

Chapter I

# ROARING THROUGH THE TWENTIES
## NORTHWESTERN OUTGROWS ITS FIRST LIBRARY

Seventy years after its opening, Northwestern University had come a long way. The school had started in Evanston in 1855, at the corner of what is now Davis and Hinman, with one building (holding classrooms, offices, library, and chapel), two faculty members, and five students. During those first years, the curriculum was limited and highly structured; students listened to lectures and read from a few standard textbooks. The early library—at first a room in the Old College building, later a larger room in University Hall—was open just a few hours a week and primarily served faculty, since students had little occasion to use books beyond the required texts.

By 1925, Northwestern was firmly established as a university. The College of Liberal Arts had been joined by schools of speech, music, engineering, and commerce in Evanston, and schools of medicine, dentistry, pharmacy, law, and commerce scattered throughout downtown Chicago. Student registration in Evanston was nearly 4,000, and, counting the Chicago schools, full-time enrollment in 1925 approached 9,500. Tuition in the College of Liberal Arts had risen to $112.50 per semester from the $45 annual fee charged in the 1850s. While the majority of students still came from Illinois, the student body represented all forty-eight states and over thirty countries outside the United States. Women students (Northwestern had been co-ed since 1869) outnumbered men in the College of Liberal Arts and in the schools of Music and Speech; overall, counting Chicago schools and part-time attendees, 1925 enrollment included over 2,800 women.

JANET OLSON
*Assistant University Archivist*

13

Students of the 1920s exit the front steps of Old College, which had been moved to the lakefront to serve as a classroom building.

As enrollment grew, the number of faculty members and academic programs expanded as well. By 1925, over two hundred full- and part-time faculty members taught in the College of Liberal Arts and Graduate School; including the Chicago schools, the total numbered over six hundred. New programs were added, and departments evolved into separate schools in response to new demands and trends. Northwestern's summer session program began in 1914. In 1921, the Medill School of Journalism emerged from the School of Commerce, and in 1926, the School of Education separated from the College of Liberal Arts, where it had been a department.

Students in the early days of Northwestern occupied their time outside the classroom with literary societies, banjo clubs, tug-of-war competitions, and the annual ceremonial burning of trigonometry books. But as the student population grew, so did the number of extracurricular activities. In an article called "The Strenuous Life in College," one student rattled off some of the dizzying array of choices awaiting the incoming freshman:

Which Frat? The Eleven? The Nine? The Five? The Crew? Debate? Y.M.C.A.? Glee Club? Settlement? Society? Club? Daily? Magazine? Annual? Stage? Class Officer? Forum? et cetera, ad infinitum

In 1925, the Women's Athletic Association (WAA) and the Men's Union (MU) were still producing separate year-end revues; the first combined WAA-MU show, *Good Morning Glory,* debuted in 1929. Members of the YWCA and YMCA had been putting on the Northwestern Circus as a benefit for the NU Settlement Association and other causes since 1908. Traditional literary societies were still popular, as were the debating and musical societies. The football team formerly known as the Purple earned a new name—the Wildcats—after a 1924 game against the University of Chicago. Dyche Stadium, named for Northwestern's longtime business manager William Dyche, opened in 1926 to host Wildcats home games. Homecoming, a tradition since 1911, was marked by a formal dance; other dances were sponsored by fraternities and sororities throughout the year. (Prior to Prohibition, some dances were held outside the four-mile limit marking the "dry" zone specified in Northwestern's charter.) All of these activities were reported on in the *Daily Northwestern* (the university's student paper since 1881), parodied in the

These cameos of daily student life appeared in the *Syllabus* yearbook.

Walter Dill Scott (1869-1955) was president of Northwestern University during a time of tremendous growth and change.

*Purple Parrot* humor magazine, and ignored or deplored in the literary magazine, the *Scrawl*.

Despite the increases in number of faculty, educational programs, and student body, no new academic buildings had been added to the Evanston campus since 1915, when Harris Hall opened—and when the student population of Northwestern University had totaled 2,500. Scattered along the lakefront were ten academic buildings, Garrett Biblical Institute, the Dearborn Observatory, the original Patten Gymnasium, a Coast Guard station, and a cluster of men's dormitories. One of the academic buildings was Old College, the first Northwestern building, which had been moved from its original location.

While the Evanston campus was experiencing a building lull, Northwestern accomplished one of its long-term goals with the opening of the Chicago campus in June 1926. The new campus, located on Chicago Avenue near the old Water Tower, consolidated the university's downtown schools from the various buildings they had previously occupied in the Loop and on the near South Side. Dedication ceremonies were held June 15–17 for the campus's new buildings: the Ward Building (housing the medical, dental, and pharmacy schools), Wieboldt Hall (for the Chicago division of the commerce, journalism, and evening classes), and Levy Mayer Hall/Elbert Gary Law Library (law school).

Construction of the new campus was made possible by an aggressive fund-raising campaign that resulted in $7 million to build and endow the Chicago schools. The "Campaign for a Greater Northwestern" was engineered by the university's president, Walter Dill Scott, a former Northwestern undergrad in liberal arts (1895) who brought a doctorate in psychology and expertise in advertising to Northwestern when he was named president in 1920. Scott steered the university through boom and bust for the next nineteen years. In addition to fund-raising for the Chicago campus, Scott initiated a campaign—"An Investment for All Time"—to increase student housing, classroom buildings, salaries, and academic programs on the Evanston campus. Between 1921 and 1930, the university's endowment increased from under $6 million to $25,526,000, and the physical plant (including both campuses) grew in value from $2,675,000 to over $16 million.

The plans for the Chicago campus and all of its buildings were designed by James Gamble Rogers, Northwestern's architect since 1922. Rogers's work at Yale, where he had designed buildings including Harkness Memorial Quadrangle (1921), had made him a prestigious name in academic architecture, and Walter Dill Scott hoped that the association of Rogers with Northwestern would bring additional attention—and donors—to the university. Rogers would ultimately design twelve buildings for Northwestern University, including the Charles Deering Memorial Library.

In September 1927, the Women's Quads, comprising fourteen sorority houses (also designed by James Gamble Rogers), opened on the Evanston campus. In his President's Report for 1927, Scott commented, "This group of buildings and that on the Chicago Campus have brought an entirely new physical element into the University, that of the architecturally balanced group. Not only the university but the cities of Chicago and Evanston have been the gainer by the sustained beauty which Mr. James Gamble Rogers has brought out in these groups." In the same report, Scott broached the pressing need for a new library in Evanston, stating that an adequate library efficiently housed is as vital to the health of any educational institution, particularly an institution attempting to encourage graduate work, as is an adequate faculty. There is nothing more discouraging to the student than being shut off from books, which must be the foundation of his work. Yet this is the situation we are approaching from the physical inability to grant the student access to the books we have.

Theodore Wesley Koch (1871–1941), university librarian from 1919 to 1941, employed persistence and vision to bring the new Deering Library into being.

The building to which Scott alluded was Lunt Library, the university's first purpose-built library, which had opened in 1894 as part of Northwestern president Henry Wade Rogers's ambitious plan to transform Northwestern into a modern university. Rogers had persuaded Orrington Lunt, one of the university's founders, to give $50,000 toward a library building; the university matched Lunt's gift with contributions and funds from its operating budget. Architect William Augustus Otis (1855–1929), who had studied at the École des Beaux-Arts in Paris and worked with Chicago architect William Le Baron Jenney, designed the three-story library structure in the Italian Renaissance style. The stacks and the reading room,

The Lunt Library circulation desk

The Lunt Library Reading Room in the 1920s was crowded with tables and card catalogs.

on the first floor, were planned to house 100,000 volumes and seat 140 students. The second floor originally held office space and a lecture room, and the smaller third floor housed the language departments. The University Guild used rooms on the second floor for meeting and exhibit space for its art collection, including objects and murals from the Columbian Exposition. By the 1920s, most of the available space in Lunt was needed for storage of a collection that had grown to over 350,000 books.

As had his predecessors at Lunt, university librarian T. W. Koch had been lobbying administrators and donors for a new building since soon after he arrived at Northwestern in 1919. In 1925, trustee Mark Cresap gently informed Koch that a new building was a "pipe dream." Koch remained undeterred. When Scott announced, in 1927, that the significant donation of the year on the Evanston campus was a $500,000 bequest from Charles Deering, Koch wrote to business manager William Dyche and to President Scott, suggesting that the university seek the support of the Deering family for "a splendid living memorial" in the form of a new library.

# Charles Deering
## (1852–1927)

*Gifted, shy, student of art and nature, collector, urbane host, large giver to hospital and educational interests:* thus was Charles Deering described on his death in 1927. The man who made the building of the Deering Library possible was a scholar and an artist, a former naval officer who became a businessman and a benefactor.

He was born in South Paris, Maine, the son of William and Abby Deering. His father, the founder and president of Deering Harvester Company, was active in Northwestern University's early development. William Deering was president of Northwestern University's board of trustees from 1897 to 1906, and donated a total of $1.2 million to the university in his lifetime, including the money to build Fisk Hall (designed by Daniel Burnham) in 1899.

Charles's brother, James (1859–1925), attended the Northwestern University Academy (the university's preparatory school) in the 1870s. James donated $1 million to Wesley Memorial Hospital (of which his father had been a founder), which became Northwestern University's

teaching hospital. James built Vizcaya, the Deering family estate in Florida, which he and Charles developed as a site for cultivating and experimenting with warm-weather plants.

Charles Deering attended the U.S. Naval Academy, graduating in 1873, and remained in the navy for twelve years, until his father asked him to join the Deering Harvester Company. After 1902, when the company merged with the McCormick Harvesting Machine Company and became International Harvester, Charles held positions on the board. Throughout his life, he pursued his interests in art as a mentor and collector (his friend the painter John Singer Sargent had once tried to persuade Deering to pursue his own painting career). He collected artwork, furniture, and books, filling homes in Spain and Evanston as well as the Florida estate. After the death of his first wife, he married Marion Whipple (1857–1943) in 1883; their children were Marion, Barbara, and Roger.

Like his father and brother, Charles was a generous benefactor to Northwestern University. He endowed

Portrait by an unknown artist

a botany professorship in his father's name, donated the Audubon *Birds of America* folios that are still the library's most important rare books, and at his death left money to Wesley Memorial Hospital, as well as the $500,000 gift to the university that became the first donation toward the new library named in his honor. His generosity to Northwestern University was continued by his widow and their three children, and the tradition has been maintained by succeeding generations.

# THE CHARLES DEERING LEGACY

Photograph of Charles Deering (undated)

The Deering family had long been supporters of Northwestern. William Deering (1826–1913), founder of the Deering Harvester Company, had been a president of the university's board of trustees, and had funded the construction of Fisk Hall (designed by the firm of Daniel Burnham) in the 1890s, among other donations. His son Charles (1852–1927) followed his father at Deering Harvester, which merged with the McCormick Harvesting Machine Company to form International Harvester in 1902. The Deering and McCormick families were further linked when Charles Deering's daughter Marion married Chauncey McCormick, great-grandson of William McCormick, a founder of the McCormick Harvesting Machine Company. Another branch of the McCormick family donated $125,000 to help establish Northwestern University's Medill School of Journalism.

The terms of Charles Deering's $500,000 bequest to Northwestern stated that the money could be used for a project of the university's choosing. Primed by Koch, the Deering family readily agreed that a library building would be a fitting tribute to Charles Deering's love of books. With additional gifts from Charles's widow and their children, the library fund totaled $1 million by 1930. Although Charles Deering's gifts to the university during his lifetime had been anonymous, the family assented when the board of trustees proposed naming the new library for him.

As soon as the Deerings' full gift was announced, university librarian Koch set off for New York, accompanied by history professor James Alton James, chair of the Library Committee of the Faculty, to meet with university architect James Gamble Rogers to discuss plans for the new Charles Deering Memorial Library.

Audubon's *The Birds of America*, 1827–38, donated to the library by Charles Deering; double-elephant folio (100 cm.), with 435 hand-colored plates

# Chapter II

# JAMES GAMBLE ROGERS
## AND THE COLLEGIATE GOTHIC ERA

RUSSELL CLEMENT
*Head of the Art Collection*

The Collegiate Gothic style, which flourished in the United States in the early twentieth century, was popular on Ivy League campuses for its association with revered English universities such as Oxford and Cambridge. It manifested and evoked the spirit of the Middle Ages, a time when learning and humanism were protected within Gothic walls and quadrangles. As bastions of traditional knowledge and as guardians of learning, Collegiate Gothic campuses spurned contemporary European modernist idioms, such as those developed at the Bauhaus and elsewhere, which were based on functionalism and clean, geometric lines of concrete and glass.

Understanding the architectural aesthetic at work in the Charles Deering Memorial Library requires reaching back to original twelfth- and thirteenth-century European Gothic architectural antecedents. Many elements of Gothic architecture converged at the abbey church of Saint-Denis near Paris, which exemplified the ideals, vision, and spirituality of Abbott Suger. Known until the Reformation as the French Style (*Opus Francigenum*), characteristic Gothic features include pointed arches, ribbed vaults, flying buttresses, and spacious clerestory and rose windows filled with stained glass. Suger's desire was to create a stunning and faith-promoting physical representation of the Heavenly New Jerusalem, a soaring, highly linear building suffused with light and color. Supplanted by Italian Renaissance architecture in the fifteenth century, Gothic architecture underwent a revival in mid-eighteenth century England, spread throughout nineteenth-century Europe, and continued to influence the design of ecclesiastical and collegiate buildings into the early twentieth century.

The Great Hall of Princeton
University's Graduate School,
built in 1910, exemplifies Cram's
Collegiate Gothic style.

# RALPH ADAMS CRAM

It was Ralph Adams Cram (1863–1942), the foremost practitioner of Gothic Revival architecture of his day, who inaugurated the modern incarnation of the style in early twentieth-century America. The Gothic style he championed was not a dry replication, but instead a vigorous resurgent architecture, adapted to the changing needs of modern society. Cram was an American Anglo-Catholic Episcopalian and latter-day Ruskinian who extolled the virtues of the Gothic style for a Christian society. He admired the early neo-Gothic architecture of H. H. Richardson and Henry Vaughan, the English neo-Gothicist who designed the National Cathedral in Washington, D.C. Cram joined these aesthetic forces to revitalize the Gothic style in America, just as McKim, Mead & White had reinvigorated classicism. Cram saw the Gothic idiom not as a dead style, but as one arrested in its development by the interjection of Renaissance classicism. Gothic architecture was not so much a collection of details as it was the embodiment of principles of truth in response to function and structural integrity. For Cram, art and religion were one. "My idea," Cram wrote in his 1936 autobiography, "was that we should set ourselves to pick up the threads of a broken tradition and strongly stand for Gothic as a style . . . that was not dead but only moribund and perfectly susceptible for an awakening to life again."

Cram's masterpieces combine the finest construction, excellent carved details, and stained-glass windows of intense saturated colors. His firm received national attention in 1903 when it won the competition for a master plan and new buildings for the U.S. Military Academy at West Point. Cram's soaring Gothic fortress fully exploits West Point's dramatic site above the Hudson River. The Cadet Chapel, an assertive, heavily proportioned free adaptation of English Gothic chapels and parish churches, rises over the parade ground as a constant reminder of militant Christianity. No better icon of Cram's integration of spiritual and architectural muscularity exists than the cross in the form of a sword hilt embellished over its main door.

Cram followed his success at West Point with the equally acclaimed design for St. Thomas Episcopal Church on Fifth Avenue in New York (1905), as well as his grand design for the nearby Cathedral of St. John the Divine (1912–41). Such high-profile building projects mark the culminating achievements of Gothic Revival in early twentieth-century America.

Cram's modernized neo-Gothicism was widely popular at private boarding schools, such as Phillips Exeter Academy in New Hampshire, as well as on college and university campuses. His educational commissions include Wheaton College, Sweet Briar College, Bryn Mawr, Mount Holyoke, Wellesley, Williams, and Rice. His best-known Collegiate Gothic buildings are at Princeton University, where he was supervising architect. Princeton's Graduate School (1910) and University Chapel (1911) are high-water marks in Anglo-American neo-Gothic residential college architecture.

In explaining his dedication to the Gothic as the most appropriate style for educational institutions, Cram wrote that the late Gothic of the colleges at Oxford and Cambridge was "the only style that absolutely expresses [the] ideals of an education that makes for culture and . . . character." The author of two dozen books and scores of magazine and journal articles on various topics, including Japanese architectural history, Cram was head of the School of Architecture at MIT, where he taught from 1914 to 1921. His passionate, albeit eclectic, medievalism was the sphere of his greatest influence. He persuaded Henry Adams to publish his *Mont Saint-Michel and Chartres* (1904) and wrote its introduction. He helped to found the Medieval Academy of America and inspired Kenneth Conant's groundbreaking work on Cluny at Harvard.

Cram returned to the image of the sword in later life, as the influence of Le Corbusier and other leading European modernists crept into the United States, much to Cram's dismay. "These things," he wrote, referring to the stripped-down elements of the new modernism, "seem to me a betrayal of trust, a vicious though unintentional assault on the basic principles of a sane and wholesome society." The modernist aesthetic, he went on, "has its own place and it may and should go for it. Its boundaries are definite and fixed, and beyond them it cannot go, for the Angel of Decency, Propriety, and Reason stands there with a flaming sword."

# JAMES GAMBLE ROGERS

ram's powerful Gothic Revivalist buildings influenced a number of architects, including Bertram Goodhue (1869–1924), a former partner who designed the Rockefeller Chapel at the University of Chicago (1918), and James Gamble Rogers (1867–1947), who built quadrangles, towers, and the new main library at Yale University (from 1917 to 1930), and similar buildings at Northwestern University.

Born in Kentucky, Rogers grew up in the boomtown of Chicago after the fire of 1871 and graduated from Yale in 1889. Before striking out on his own in 1891 with his brother, John Arthur Rogers, James Gamble Rogers gained valuable experience at the two firms that stood at the core of the Chicago School. He began his architectural career in the Chicago office of William Le Baron Jenney, despite having no formal training. Jenney's office was a fertile breeding ground for successful Chicago architects. Fellow alumni included William Otis, Louis Sullivan, William Holabird, Martin Roche, and Daniel Burnham. Jenney and his chief designer, William Brice Mundie (whom Rogers later acknowledged as a mentor), were adept at transforming an amalgamation of romantic styles (neo-Gothic, neo-Romantic, etc.) and academic commissions into attractive, well-constructed, and well-engineered buildings that came in at cost.

James Gamble Rogers

After two years, Rogers left Jenney's office for the dynamic practice of Burnham & Root, where he supervised the Ashland Block (1892), at the time the largest building project in the office and an important addition to downtown Chicago. Most notable for directing architectural planning of the 1893 World's Columbian Exposition held in Chicago, as well as for the visionary 1909 *Plan of Chicago*, Daniel Burnham established the concept of urban planning in the United States and influenced the redesign of cities worldwide.

Once established on their own, the Rogers brothers' first commission was the Lees Building in Chicago (demolished 1969), constructed on a fireproofed steel frame clad with pressed brick and terra-cotta. The Rand McNally Company, in its compendium of Chicago buildings, called it "the best lighted office building in the city."

Rogers's first commission, the Lees Building in downtown Chicago, was pictured in an illustrated guide to the city for visitors to the World's Columbian Exhibition in 1893.

The Evanston Public Library at 1703 Orrington Avenue, designed by James Gamble Rogers and Charles Philips, opened in 1908. It was replaced by a new building in 1961, which was in turn replaced by the current building in 1994.

Rogers's Harkness House at One East Seventy-fifth Street in Manhattan was designed as the private home of Edward and Mary Harkness.

Well on his way to becoming a successful Chicago architect, in 1892 Rogers enrolled at the École des Beaux-Arts in Paris, where he won medals in architecture and construction and graduated with honors in 1898. His decision to leave Chicago likely hinged on the realization that further academic training was a prerequisite for receiving the important civic and business commissions he craved. Rogers returned to Chicago and maintained an office with his brother until 1905. They designed residences on the North Shore and the Winton Block at Michigan Avenue and Thirteenth Street (1904), which was noted for its early use of reinforced concrete frame technology. In 1905, Rogers designed Belfield Hall for the School of Education at the University of Chicago, followed a year later by its gymnasium (since demolished). He also designed the Evanston Public Library with Charles A. Philips in 1906 (since demolished).

He was thirty-eight years old, newly married, managing a thriving practice in Chicago, and ready to assume a central position in the city's architectural community. At the same time, he was beginning to receive commissions outside of Chicago, and influential friends from Yale lived in and around New York. In 1905, Rogers moved his office to New York and entered into a short-lived practice with Herbert D. Hale. The prospect of larger commissions may have lured him into making such a large geographic jump.

The building that made Rogers's mark in New York was a house commissioned by the client who shaped the rest of his career, Edward S. Harkness (1874–1940). The design of Harkness House, on the corner of Fifth Avenue and Seventy-fifth Street, was a major step up for Rogers and put his work visibly at the center of New York's social world. The mansion pleased both Harkness and major architectural critics of the day. Designated a landmark in 1967, it is currently the home of Harkness's philanthropic Commonwealth Fund. A wealthy philanthropist and Yale graduate (1897), Harkness gave away $129 million before his death. He used some of his money to help construct major buildings for educational and religious institutions—Yale, Harvard, Columbia, Atlanta College, Columbia-Presbyterian Medical Center, Colgate Rochester Divinity School—as well as regional health centers across rural America. Rogers became Harkness's favorite architect, and he designed the great majority of these buildings.

Interior view of the Rogers and Philips Evanston Public Library

Northwestern rejected Rogers's first design for a Gothic library, saying it too closely resembled his Sterling Memorial Library, then under construction at Yale.

Harkness Tower rises over the Memorial Quadrangle at Yale, now the site of Saybrook College and Branford College.

The development of Harkness's interest in buildings defined Rogers's career from 1916 until Harkness's death in 1940. Harkness's longtime friend and financial advisor, Sam Fisher, a lawyer who practiced in New Haven and another Yale graduate, was a friend of Rogers and probably introduced the men. The three became close friends and frequently traveled together. Harkness would often set as a condition of his gift for a new academic or medical building the institution's agreement to hire Rogers for the project. It is therefore no coincidence that Rogers's works are abundant at Yale, Columbia, and other institutions that Harkness supported. Rogers rose to national prominence when he won the competitions for the post offices and courthouses in New Orleans (1908–15) and New Haven (1911–19), hailed for their scholarly use of Roman and Renaissance precedents.

With his designs for Harkness Tower and Harkness Memorial Quadrangle at Yale (1916–21), Rogers moved fully into the Collegiate Gothic style. For the Yale commissions, Rogers hired E. Donald Robb, a designer who had worked for Ralph Adams Cram and Bertram Goodhue. Robb specialized in moody renderings that converted the proposed buildings into evocative medieval images. Rogers was an expedient latecomer to neo-Gothicism, and his new buildings at Yale have been criticized for failing to convincingly reproduce the centuries-old patina of Cambridge and Oxford. Rogers's surface Gothicism could hardly have pleased Cram. But Rogers did not share Cram's belief that a building's exterior should forthrightly declare its structure. For Rogers and his academic clients, function often trumped neo-Gothic decorations, which sometimes appear as superficial stylistic additions. In a letter written in 1919, Rogers rejected Cram's insistence on archaeological neo-Gothicism in favor of a more experientially based, pragmatic approach. In his mind, he was not a copyist caught up in traditions for their own sake:

> As far as traditions go, I hope that the only traditions governing us will be Yale traditions and our country's traditions. Architecturally we will, I know, keep our effects as essential and not the traditions. Of course we will have to have architectural traditions because in most cases there is no other way of getting the desired effect except by employing the traditions which we use only because in those cases they are necessary to get the effect. It does seem awfully hollow and servilely cringing to use a tradition that means nothing to us.

Rogers submitted this neo-Gothic entry to the 1922 design competition for the Chicago *Tribune*'s new building on Michigan Avenue, along with 260 other famous and aspiring architects. The winning design—also neo-Gothic, down to its set of flying buttresses—came from John Mead Howells and Raymond Hood.

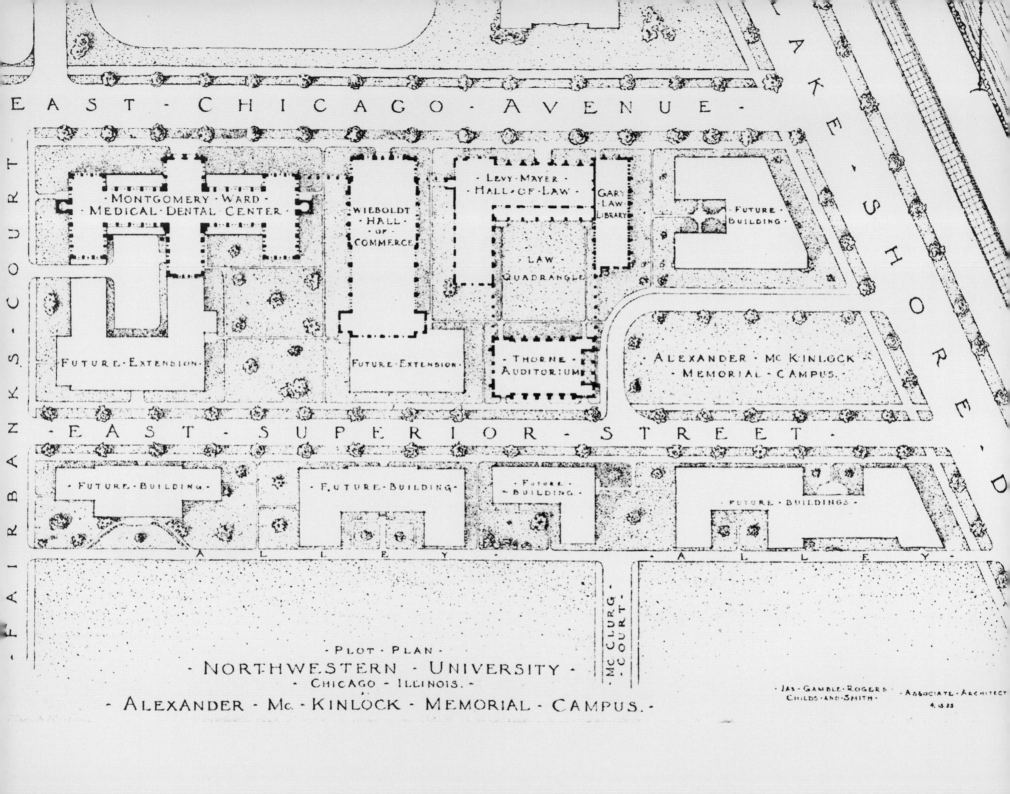

The finished Chicago campus included (from left to right) the Montgomery Ward Building (Medical/Dental School), Wieboldt Hall (School of Commerce), Levy Mayer Hall (Law School) and Gary Law Library, and the Thorne Auditorium.

The peculiarities of Rogers's illusory or faux-Gothic are most evident on the exteriors and in eye-catching decorative details, which seep through the rest of his structures. For buildings such as the Harkness Quadrangle, for example, Rogers conceived an assemblage of "medieval" details separately from the plan, so as not to hinder the building's modern functional arrangement. This strategy and formula became the hallmark of his Collegiate Gothic projects, which are, in the words of architectural historian Aaron Betsky, "still wonderful chimeras of Neo-Gothic villages of forms strewn together with ornamental narratives along revelatory paths and constructed on steel skeletons with double-loaded corridors." Rogers had found an idiom that added historical and cultural imagery to functional structures.

By the time he received the commission for the Charles Deering Memorial Library, Rogers had designed dozens of Collegiate Gothic buildings, including, most notably, Yale's Sterling Memorial Library (1924–31). In 1912, he was offered the position of consulting architect at Yale, which he declined. He was appointed campus architect and master planner at Yale in 1920, a position he held for over a decade. Designs for later campus buildings, in particular the Tower at Yale's Hall of Graduate Studies (1930–32), were further experiments in his modernized Gothic style.

As Northwestern's architect, Rogers drew up the plan for the new Chicago campus, as well as the designs for each building.

# ROGERS AT NORTHWESTERN

lthough he was appointed campus architect by president Walter Dill Scott in 1922, Rogers never produced a comprehensive master plan. President Scott wanted to model Northwestern's buildings on Ivy League campuses. Rogers instead designed a series of structures that incrementally changed the character of the Evanston campus. Rogers's proposal for the nascent downtown Chicago campus called for a series of tall blocks marching down Chicago Avenue, each housing one of the professional schools. The tallest of the structures, the medical school and hospital, was to be closest to Michigan Avenue. Over the next decade, this scheme was constructed almost exactly as proposed. Buildings Rogers designed for the Chicago campus included the Montgomery Ward Memorial Building (1926), Wieboldt Hall of Commerce (1926), Levy Mayer Hall of Law and Elbert H. Gary Library of Law (1927), George R. Thorne Hall (1932), and Abbott Hall (1940).

In Evanston, he designed Sorority Quadrangle (1927), Dyche Stadium (1926), Hobart Hall (1929), Rogers Hall (1929), Charles Deering Memorial Library (1932), Willard Hall (1938), Scott Hall (1940), and Lutkin Hall (1941). Other proposed buildings, including a university chapel, were never realized. While these buildings serve as focal points for the development of the campus, Rogers only inconclusively defined the character and spatial organization of Northwestern University before he was replaced as campus architect in 1943. In terms of its style and grandeur, the Charles Deering Memorial Library was the most important building Rogers designed at Northwestern University.

Exterior of Levy Mayer Hall (Northwestern University Law School), showing the Cloister Garden

### SOURCES CONSULTED

Anthony, Ethan. *The Architecture of Ralph Adams Cram and His Office.* New York: W. W. Norton, 2007.

Betsky, Aaron. *James Gamble Rogers and the Architecture of Pragmatism.* New York: Architectural History Foundation; Cambridge, Mass.: MIT Press, 1994.

Miller, Rod. *West Point U.S. Military Academy: An Architectural Tour.* New York: Princeton Architectural Press, 2002.

Shand-Tucci, Douglass. *Ralph Adams Cram: Life and Architecture.* Amherst, Mass.: University of Massachusetts Press, 1995–2005. 2 vols.

Walker, Gay. *Bonawit, Stained Glass and Yale.* Wilsonville, Ore.: Wildwood, 2000.

Wyllie, Romy. *Bertram Goodhue: His Life and Residential Architecture.* New York: W. W. Norton, 2007.

The entrance to Rogers's Wieboldt Hall (School of Commerce) is a virtual primer of high Gothic elements, including the tympanum of its pointed archway, recessed trefoil windows with tracery, pointed pilasters and domed capitals, statue niches, and strongly perpendicular orientation.

35

With its monumental keep and large lancet windows, Rogers's Scott Hall (1940) evokes the structure of a Norman fortress—and an earlier phase of Gothic style.

Rogers's Lutkin Hall, built for the School of Music and named for the school's founder, Peter Christian Lutkin, exhibits an eclectic mixture of Gothic and non-Gothic architectural elements.

The Women's Quads opened on the Evanston campus in 1924.

An early Rogers proposal for
Deering Library showed a
Georgian design.

# Chapter III

# A HAVEN FOR STUDENTS
## THE DEERING VISION MADE REAL

The first design Rogers produced for the new library at Northwestern proposed a Gothic structure that university librarian Theodore Koch felt too closely resembled Sterling Memorial Library at Yale. Koch responded with a detailed plan of what he considered the most efficient layout of the library. Rogers countered with a Georgian scheme, consisting of a simple form with a central tower, which would be both appropriate for the use and relatively inexpensive to build. Rogers's first sketches "left the Building Committee cold and unresponsive," according to Koch, who was particularly unimpressed with them.

The building committee, led by President Scott, insisted on a neo-Gothic library of the sort that Rogers had become known for. After much back-and-forth correspondence among Scott, Rogers, and Koch, Rogers offered to redo the plan in a "simplified Gothic" style. This design would echo elements of the King's College Chapel at Cambridge, in particular its eleven identical bays, separated by buttresses tapering toward the roof, the full-story leaded glass windows with pointed arches, and the pairs of octagonal towers at the north and south ends. In the end, President Scott obtained his neo-Gothic monument and Koch got a simplified design that in many ways resembled his initial functional layout.

The proposed new building was to be two hundred feet long and forty feet wide, two stories tall, with a basement and six tiers of book stacks. Speaking practically, the design would be flexible enough to adapt to changing needs, and wings could be added to the north, south, and east to expand the library's capacity in the future.

JANET OLSON

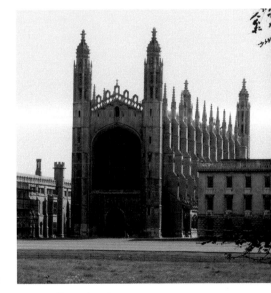

King's College Chapel in Cambridge, England, influenced Rogers's design for Deering Library.

# KOCH'S VISION FOR THE NEW LIBRARY

T. W. Koch threw himself with joyful energy into planning the library he had dreamed of for so long. As Rogers worked on his designs, Koch visited numerous academic libraries and consulted with additional university librarians and experts by mail. The stamp of his taste and ideas was visible in every aspect of the project.

Koch expressed his vision for the new structure and its functions in numerous articles. In a two-issue newsletter, the *Charles Deering Library Bulletin*, Koch addressed topics ranging from a defense of the Gothic style to the configuration of the plumbing, from the meaning of the carved inscriptions to the specifications for chairs and tables, and from advances in library technology to anticipation of patrons' feelings of awe and inspiration upon entering the reading room.

While Koch stressed the practical, modern features of the design, he could not resist frequent references to its aesthetic and abstract aspects, especially the feelings that the building was meant to evoke. His conception of the library was holistic—he worked to bring out both the concrete and the metaphorical implications of the design at every turn. To Koch, the appeal of the Gothic was in its emotional and dynamic elements. Gothic architecture, he wrote, "is essentially emotional, whereas classic architecture is intellectual . . . Gothic architecture is dynamic. . . . If you knock out the flying buttresses the vaults overthrow the walls. If you knock out the vaults the buttresses will push the wall in." The combination of the dynamic and the emotional made the Gothic appropriate for an academic building, especially a library, because "no other architectural style, unless it be the Greek, has expressed more adequately the upward-reaching of man's spirit."

The site chosen for the library, along the crest of a low ridge paralleling Sheridan Road, had previously been occupied by Heck Hall, a yellow-brick dormitory used by the "Bibs," as Garrett Biblical Institute students were called. Heck Hall had burned down in 1914. The buildings near the site were Memorial Hall to the north,

A tribute to Charles Deering in Koch's "occasionally" published *Charles Deering Library Bulletin* pointed out that "the tact, courtesy, and affability which had endeared [him] to his classmates so attracted General and Mrs. Ulysses S. Grant that they invited him to serve as their personal escort on their tour around the world."

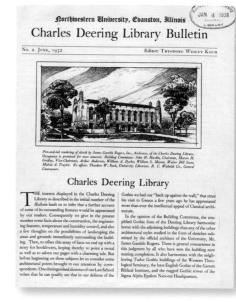

The second—and last—issue of the *Bulletin* included an engineer's exhaustive description of the heating and ventilating system, a thirteen-page "Tale for Bibliophiles" translated from the German by Koch, and a personal note inserted on Koch's own stationery, soliciting books from the personal collections of his readers for the new library's Browsing Room.

The site chosen for Deering Library had originally been occupied by Heck Hall, which was destroyed by a fire in 1914.

Koch used the *Charles Deering Library Bulletin* to express his opinions on design details, including the perfect furniture finish and the proper construction of chairs.

which housed the commerce and journalism schools, and Annie May Swift to the south, home of the School of Speech (known as the School of Oratory until 1921). The book stacks of the new library would face the Lake Michigan shore, with the facade fronting Sheridan Road, although set back about four hundred feet from the street. President Scott saw the new library as the centerpiece and architectural keynote for a future grouping of buildings, to be designed by Rogers, that would transform the Evanston campus. Koch, whose aspirations for the new library matched those of President Scott in scope, agreed that this site would provide the thousands of people passing along Sheridan Road with a "glimpse of the Evanston campus of the future."

# CONSTRUCTION

eering Library was built, decorated, and trimmed with many varieties of stone and wood from all over the country, and despite its construction during the early years of the Great Depression, the finishing touches—carvings, paneling, and stained-glass window insets—evoke an impression of opulence.

The exterior is of Lannon stone, a very hard limestone from Wisconsin, trimmed with gray Bedford limestone from Indiana on the corners. The stone was shipped to Joliet, Illinois, and hand cut (due to its machine-resistant density) in the workshop of Adam Groth & Sons. (The same Lannon stone was used in the Women's Quadrangle and the Seabury-Western Theological Seminary.) Bedford limestone was also used on walls and trim on the library's interior, varied with ocher-toned Ohio sandstone. Granite slabs for ground-level window ledges and the steps leading to the main entrance came from Cold Spring, Minnesota. The travertine marble for the inside staircases was quarried in Winona, Minnesota, while gray marble from Tennessee was used in other parts of the building. The loggia was paved with George Washington sandstone from Alexandria, Virginia. Buff-colored pressed brick from Pennsylvania was used on the walls of the ground floor and corridors. Concrete floors were overlaid with terrazzo on the ground floor and Romany red clay tiles on the first floor (in other places, linoleum or rubber flooring was installed). Aside from stone, about 65,000 square feet of Appalachian white oak from Louisville, Kentucky, kiln dried and wire brushed, was used for wood trim, doors, and bookcases.

Behind the solidly medieval surfaces, modern materials and building methods were employed, although often disguised. As Koch said, "Since . . . Gothic architecture is a style of continual growth it is fitting that the Gothic now being employed at Northwestern University should depart somewhat from the older forms in order to conform to the materials now being used, [and] to the recent developments in construction." The majestic ceiling in the main reading room on the second floor was

Early stage of the construction process, looking south (in the background: center, Annie May Swift; far right, University Hall)

CHAS. DEERING LIBRAR
NORTHWESTERN UNIVERS
EVANSTON, ILLINOIS
JAS. GAMBLE ROGERS, ARCH
R. C. WIEBOLDT, CONTRACT
DATE JAN·11·1932 NEG. NO.

Testing the concrete pilings

The site as it looked on January 11, 1932—the day before the cornerstone ceremony

supported by steel and cement beams, painted to look like wood. Steel beams also supported the window frames and the buttresses that defined the Gothic style.

Inside and out, every surface and finish was carefully chosen and embellished. Plastered ceilings were painted and stenciled in medieval style. Wood trim included ceiling beams, linen-fold paneling on walls and wainscoting, and bas-relief and three-dimensional sculptures. Stone over the arches on the exterior, and as corbels, pillars, and trim inside, was carved with inscriptions or figures. Sixty-eight stained-glass medallions were set into the huge multipaned windows on the first and second floors of the building.

Both René Paul Chambellan, the sculptor who designed the wood and stone carvings, and G. Owen Bonawit, the designer of the stained-glass medallions, had worked with James Gamble Rogers on other projects. The team had managed to inject humor and fancy into the design elements of their previous collaborations. When it came to choosing motifs for the Charles Deering Library, they found an eager co-conspirator in bibliophile Koch, whose traditional tastes and appreciation of craftsmanship were accompanied by a strong whimsical streak. Koch threw himself, his staff, and the books in the library's collections into the task of selecting design motifs that reflected—sometimes in a humorous way—the educational aspect of the building, with references to culture, literature, history, and the academic tradition.

By February 22, 1932, the arched front doors and vaulted lobby ceiling were taking shape.

The new library rising on the
lakeshore, April 28, 1932

The windowless shell of the new building, May 26, 1932

Looking south, with Annie May Swift, Fisk, the heating plant, and Old College in the background, May 12, 1932

Craftsmen working on the library's
ornamental carvings

# CARVINGS, STATUES, AND INSCRIPTIONS

American sculptor René Paul Chambellan (1893–1955) studied at the École des Beaux-Arts and at the Académie Julian in Paris. A leading practioner of what was called the French modern style, he specialized in architectural sculpture.

For his work on Deering Library, Chambellan created plaster models for the carvings, sent them to Rogers for approval, and then commissioned the artisans at Groth & Sons to carve the stone in Joliet, Illinois. Additional carving and finishing was done on-site in Evanston. Carved motifs included symbols of knowledge: an owl, a lamp, a pen, books, a scroll, an hourglass. Stone or wood borders of carved vines, fruit, and flowers were used liberally. Of Chambellan's many creations, the ones most fondly associated with Deering Library were the largest—the three-dimensional figures of a monk and an Arab scholar that are seated at the turns of the staircases leading up to the second level of the building, statues representing the spread of religious and scientific knowledge in medieval times. Bas-relief portraits of Charles Deering, T. W.

Northwestern's initial N, carved in wood over the entrance to the Reading Room

Koch, and Walter Dill Scott and the seals of the State of Illinois and Northwestern University were also prominently placed. Stone mice crept into stone books, impish reading figures served as corbels to support beams, and three-dimensional wooden animals, inspired by *Aesop's Fables*, guarded the doors into the reading rooms.

Koch gave much time and thought to selecting the inscriptions carved at strategic points throughout the building. For the cornerstone, he chose a phrase found on Roman libraries: *Nutrimentum spiritus*—"Food for the mind." The north and south exterior arches feature the proverbs "The fountain of wisdom flows through books" and "Happy is the man that findeth wisdom." Inside, carved mottos defined the purpose of the library and described the work of the scholar. Framing the interior entrance was the injunction *Aut legere scribenda: aut scribere legenda* (Either to read something worthy of being written, or to write something worth being read). At the top of the staircase on the second floor, researchers were reminded of the time-consuming process of sifting through sources and discerning the best ones, with the inscriptions *Inter folia fructus* (Among the leaves, fruit) and *Non multa, sed bona* (Not many, but good). Even the fireplace in the university librarian's office had its motto: "Old wood to burn, old books to read."

Bas-relief of T. W. Koch under the Northwestern University seal

Part of a carved inscription inside the front door exhorting students "either to read something worthy of being written, or to write something worth being read"

51

Arab scholar at the turn of the
south staircase

Monk at the turn of the north staircase

*I well remember the thrill and awe of entering the new library in 1933. The depth of the Great Depression made such an edifice doubly impressive. It opened at a time when faith in the future of the university was badly needed.*

JEAN WYNEKEN HARDY, CLASS OF 1933

The carved and beamed ceiling of the second-floor concourse, with a corbel in the shape of a bookish imp supporting the beam

53

*Aesop's Fables* provided much of the inspiration for the whimsical carved wooden animals perched on doorways and ledges.

# STAINED GLASS

Owen Bonawit (1891–1971) apprenticed in his uncle's stained-glass workshop, and by 1918 had established his own firm in New York. His commissions included windows and medallions at Yale and Duke universities, and in churches, office buildings, and homes.

Bonawit's designs for the sixty-eight stained-glass medallions in the Deering windows were based on suggestions made by Koch and library staff, using books and manuscripts from the library's collections, as well as from the artist's own knowledge and imagination. The result was an eclectic assortment of subjects drawn from literature, fable, philosophy, world religions, and history. Most of the medallions were done in subdued monochromatic tones, since Koch felt that excessive use of colored stained glass would be garish.

Medallion images were grouped in the library's rooms by theme. The windows in the reading room on the north side of the main level pictured the history of the Midwest, with portraits of Native Americans, French explorers, and Lincoln. Figures representing ancient Hindu, Roman, Greek, Hebrew, Assyrian, Chinese, and Egyptian culture were placed in the windows on the northeast end. The seminar room windows along the south wall held printers' marks and seals from American and British universities—including King's College Chapel, Cambridge, the inspiration for Deering Library's design.

In some cases, the stained-glass images reflected the specific purpose of the room. In the Commerce Reading Room on the south side of the main level, imagery was drawn from transportation and industry, with an emphasis on the Midwest: medallions depicted an Indian fur trader, a Conestoga wagon, a locomotive, a Great Lakes steamer, and an airplane, in addition to a binder, and a harvester and thresher—produced by the Deering-McCormick family company. Images of medieval copyists were placed in the librarians' workroom on the south side of the second floor. Appropriately for the window in the order department, a medieval bibliophile perched on a massive pile of books. On the north side of the second floor, Don Quixote watched over the secretary's desk in the administrative offices.

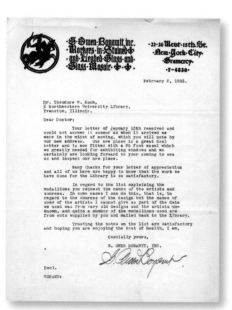

A letter on G. Owen Bonawit's Gothic letterhead about the designs used for the window medallions

*In the summer following my senior year at Northwestern, I was secretary to the assistant librarian, David Jolly. His office was adjacent to the head librarian, Jens Nyholm, and it was there I viewed a valuable addition to Deering, The Book of Hours. I used to look out the large leaded window beside my desk and watch my brand-new husband, John, with a burlap bag across his shoulder. Newly graduated from NU, and on his way to doing graduate work at Yale, he worked for Buildings and Grounds that summer, picking up trash with a long pointed stick. At summer's end, Mr. Jolly took us down to Trader Vic's in Chicago for a fancy dinner—a rare treat for the newlyweds.*

BARBARA FOSTER SCHUTZ, CLASS OF 1954

The former university librarian's office, now the Beck Angling Collection Room, as it looks today

The medallions in the windows of the great Reading Room were meant to inspire the students who studied there. The philosopher Lao-tzu stood beside the gods Brahma and Vishnu, the goddess Artemis, the angel Gabriel, and French hero Roland. Also depicted were scenes from the *Arabian Nights*, Hans Christian Andersen, Shakespeare's *A Midsummer Night's Dream*, and *The Rubaiyat of Omar Khayyam*. Symbols of the medieval trivium (Logic, Grammar, and Rhetoric) represented the foundations of a medieval university education. And the elusive Holy Grail was placed in one of the windows of the Treasure (Rare Book) Room. Cards identifying the medallion images and the sources from which they were drawn were originally placed in holders beside each of the windows; sadly, all but a few of these have disappeared over the years.

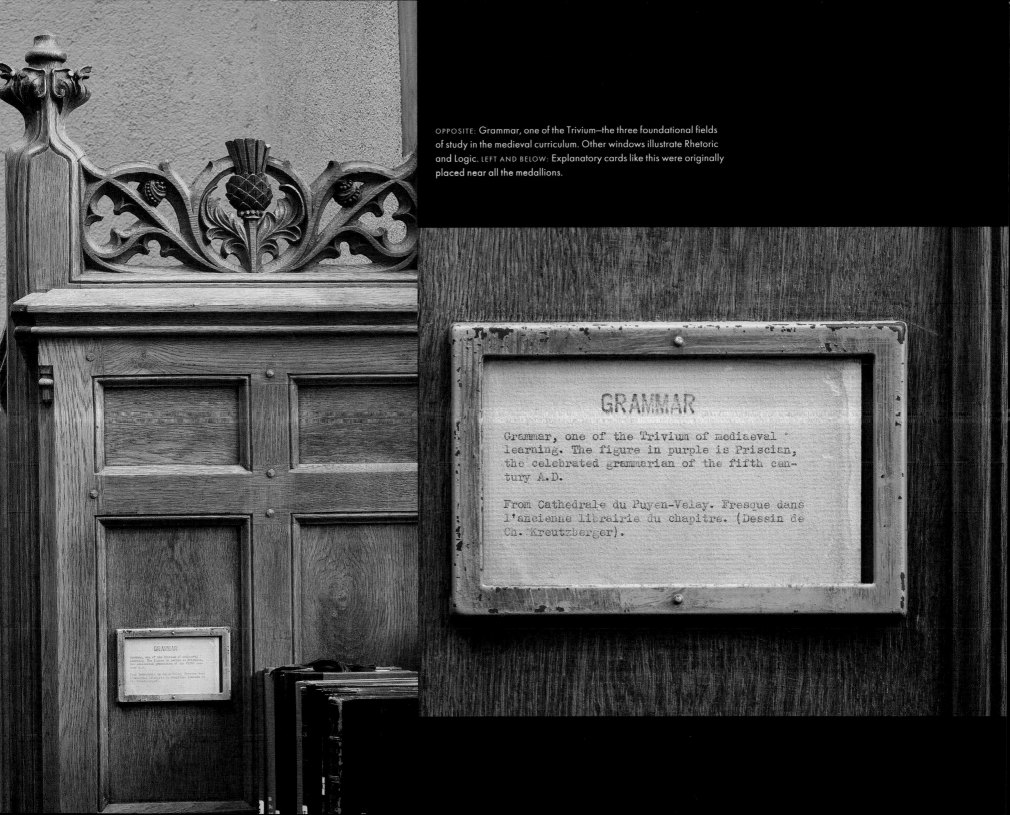

OPPOSITE: Grammar, one of the Trivium—the three foundational fields of study in the medieval curriculum. Other windows illustrate Rhetoric and Logic. LEFT AND BELOW: Explanatory cards like this were originally placed near all the medallions.

## GRAMMAR

Grammar, one of the Trivium of mediaeval learning. The figure in purple is Priscian, the celebrated grammarian of the fifth century A.D.

From Cathédrale du Puyen-Velay. Fresque dans l'ancienne librairie du chapitre. (Dessin de Ch. Kreutzberger).

# The Deering Window Medallions

Indian village

| | TITLE | CURRENT LOCATION |
|---|---|---|
| SECOND FLOOR | Jacques Marquette (French Jesuit missionary) | Music Library, Main Reading Room |
| | Robert Cavelier La Salle (French traveler, explored Mississippi) | Music Library, Main Reading Room |
| | Pontiac (Ottawa Indian chief) | Music Library, Main Reading Room |
| | George Rogers Clark (American general and explorer) | Music Library, Main Reading Room |
| | Black Hawk (American Indian chief) | Music Library, Main Reading Room |
| | Tecumtha (Shawnee Indian chief) | Music Library, Main Reading Room |
| | Abraham Lincoln | Music Library, Main Reading Room |
| | Hindu history and culture: Emperor Djahir-e-din Mohammed at the head of invading army | Music Library, West Reading Room |
| | Roman history and culture: Roman legions crossing bridge over Trojan column | Music Library, West Reading Room |
| | Greek history and culture: Theseus, Athena, and Amphitrite | Music Library, West Reading Room |
| | Hebrew history and culture: King Joash shooting arrow of deliverance | Music Library, West Reading Room |
| | Assyrian history and culture: King Assour-akh-bal, 2500 B.C.E. | Music Library, West Reading Room |
| | Chinese history and culture: Chariot of ancient Chinese emperor | Music Library, West Reading Room |
| | Egyptian history and culture: King Ramses the Great, nineteenth dynasty | Music Library, West Reading Room |
| | Airplane | Listening Center |
| | Great Lakes steamer | Listening Center |
| | Early locomotive (the Menomonee, first locomotive west of Cleveland, 1852) | Listening Center |
| | Conestoga wagon | Listening Center |
| | Horse-drawn McCormick-Deering twine binder | Listening Center |
| | No. 20 McCormick-Deering harvester and thresher | Listening Center |
| | Indian fur trader, Great Lakes region | Listening Center |
| | Cambridge University coat of arms | Music Library offices* |

*in a private office, not accessible to the public*

| TITLE | CURRENT LOCATION |
| --- | --- |
| Oxford University coat of arms | Music Library offices* |
| Oxford University arms enclosed in cartouche | Music Library offices* |
| Printer's mark, Robert Copland, Printer at Sign of Rose Garland | Music Library offices* |
| Kings College Chapel, Cambridge, coat of arms | Music Library offices* |
| Woodcut from Albrecht Dürer | Music Library offices* |
| Printer's mark, Crato Mylius (German printer) | Music Library offices* |
| Printer's mark, Andro Myllar (Scottish printer) | Music Library offices* |
| Printer's marks, Milanese printer Gian Giacomo di Legnano and French printer Antoine Vérard | Music Library offices* |
| Indian village | Music Library, Main Reading Room (bay window) |
| Indian chief (Moto Tope, chief of the Mandans) | Music Library, Main Reading Room (bay window) |
| Psalters of Robert de Lisle and Peterborough Abe (six episodes in the life of Christ) | Beck Angler Room (Special Collections office)* |
| Don Quixote reading *A Romance of Chivalry* | Special Collections office* |
| Kneeling bowman | Special Collections office* |
| Princeton University seal | Special Collections Reading Room |
| Yale University seal | Special Collections Reading Room |
| Harvard University seal | Special Collections Reading Room |
| Printer's marks of Gotardus de Pont and Jacobus Paucidrapius de Burgofranco | Special Collections Reading Room (bay window) |
| Holy Grail from *Le Morte d'Arthur* | Art Collection, north end |
| The Trivium: Rhetoric | Art Collection, north end |
| The Trivium: Grammar | Art Collection, north end |
| Genii from the *Arabian Nights* | Art Collection, north end |
| | *\* in a private office, not accessible to the public* |

THIRD FLOOR

Don Quixote

# The Deering Window Medallions

| | TITLE | CURRENT LOCATION |
|---|---|---|
| THIRD FLOOR | "The Galoshes of Fortune," Hans Christian Andersen's *Fairy Tales* | Art Collection |
| | Angel Gabriel | Art Collection |
| | Brahma, the Creator | Art Collection |
| | Roland fighting the Saracens | Art Collection |
| | In memoriam, Tennyson: "Man dies nor is there hope in dust" | Art Collection |
| | Lao-tzu, founder of Taoism | Art Collection |
| | Vishnu, the Preserver | Art Collection |
| | Artemis, Greek hunter-goddess | Art Collection |
| | *Midsummer Night's Dream*, Shakespeare, act II | Art Collection |
| | The North Wind from *Norske Folkeeventyr* | Art Collection, south end |
| | The Trivium: Logic | Art Collection, south end |
| | The Quadrivium: Music | Art Collection, south end |
| | *Rubaiyat* of Omar Khayyam, verse 17 | Art Collection, south end |
| | Greenland falcon, warlike crested eagle, and Goliath heron | Art Librarian's office* |
| | Bibliophile | Art Librarian's office* |
| | "Ecrivain au travail a la fin du Moyen Age" | Architecture Reading Room |
| | Sir Thomas Bodley, English diplomat and scholar | Architecture Reading Room |
| | Illuminator of the Middle Ages | Architecture Reading Room |
| | "Atelier de Copistes au Moyen Age" | Architecture Reading Room |
| | Mark of John Rastell, English printer of London | Architecture Reading Room |
| | Aldine anchor mark used by Paulus Manutius, Venetian | Architecture Reading Room |

*\* in a private office, not accessible to the public*

Illuminator of the Middle Ages

Owen Bonawit's original sketches for
three medallions: Abraham Lincoln,
Goliath heron, and Artemis

## INTERIOR LAYOUT

The new library's interior spaces were as carefully thought out as its design elements. There were several reading rooms with different functions, seminar rooms for classroom use, offices and workrooms for library staff, public space for exhibits, and carrel space for faculty and graduate students—along with the behind-the-scenes tiers of book stacks. Koch was particularly proud of the open layout of the floors, which simplified supervision as well as navigation, so that "no elaborate guide to the building nor direction signs will be needed. There is no danger of a freshman getting lost in a labyrinth of dark corridors."

Broad steps, perfect for sitting, led from Deering Meadow to the loggia of the new building; impressive carved doors opened into the entry area on the main level. The main floor lobby, with its low stenciled and beamed ceiling, contained wall-mounted and freestanding exhibit cases. This level held three reserve reading rooms—two on the north side of the lobby, and one, for the School of Commerce library, on the south side. Five seminar rooms extended along the south wall.

Up the double flight of stairs (past either the carved monk on the north side or the Arab scholar on the south side of the staircase landing) was another lobby on the second level, this one containing the circulation/delivery desk and card catalog. The card catalog space was designed for over 2,160 drawers—enough room for two million catalog cards.

The focal point of the new library was the Reading Room, which filled the entire west side of the second floor. This space exemplified Koch's faith in the inspirational effects of Gothic style, with its high vaulted ceilings, carved decorations, tables and chairs to seat nearly three hundred readers, massive wooden reference desk, nineteen of the stained-glass medallions in enormous arched windows, and bookcases filled with nearly ten thousand reference volumes. At the south end of the Reading Room, the Browsing Room—one of Koch's pet ideas—was furnished with comfortable chairs and with bookcases containing "several thousand volumes selected for their cultural value" for students' leisure reading. Most of the Browsing Room books were gifts from alumni and other donors.

The original floor plan for the ground floor, with its spacious Staff Room that included a resting room outfitted with beds

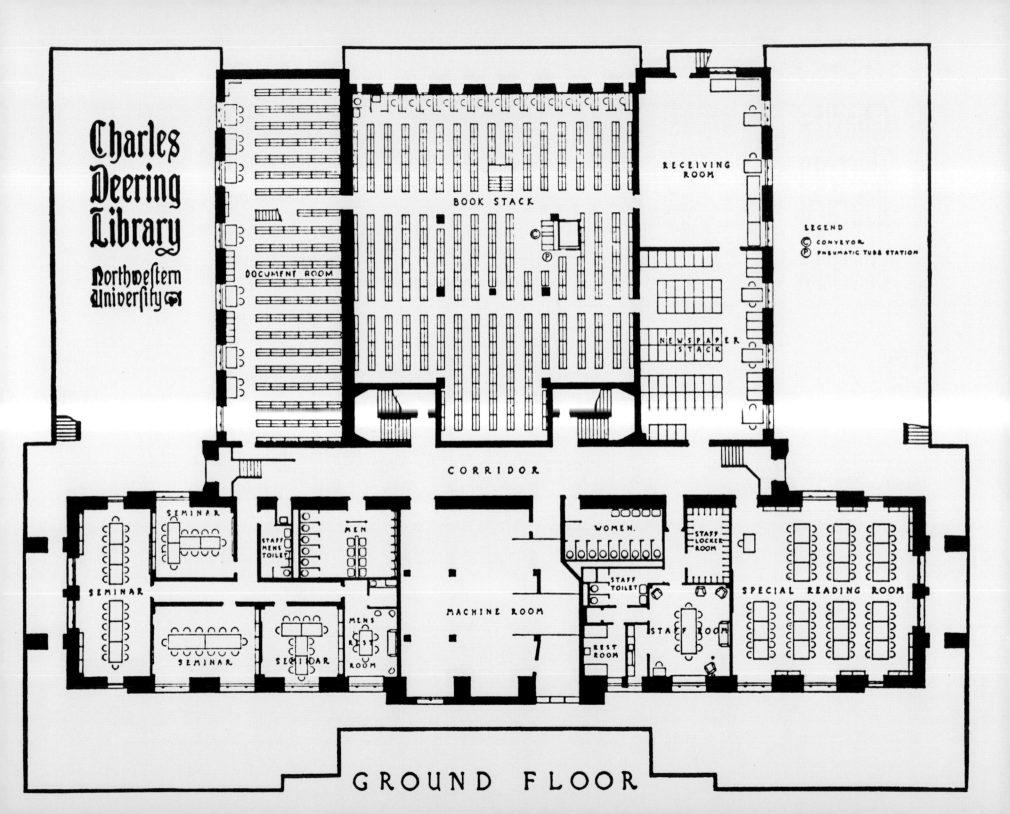

Charles
Deering
Library

Northwestern
University

DOCUMENT ROOM

BOOK STACK

RECEIVING
ROOM

LEGEND
Ⓒ CONVEYOR
Ⓟ PNEUMATIC TUBE STATION

NEWSPAPER
STACK

CORRIDOR

SEMINAR

SEMINAR

SEMINAR

SEMINAR

STAFF
MENS
TOILET

MEN

MENS
REST
ROOM

MACHINE ROOM

WOMEN.

STAFF
TOILET

REST
ROOM

STAFF
LOCKER
ROOM

STAFF ROOM

SPECIAL READING ROOM

GROUND FLOOR

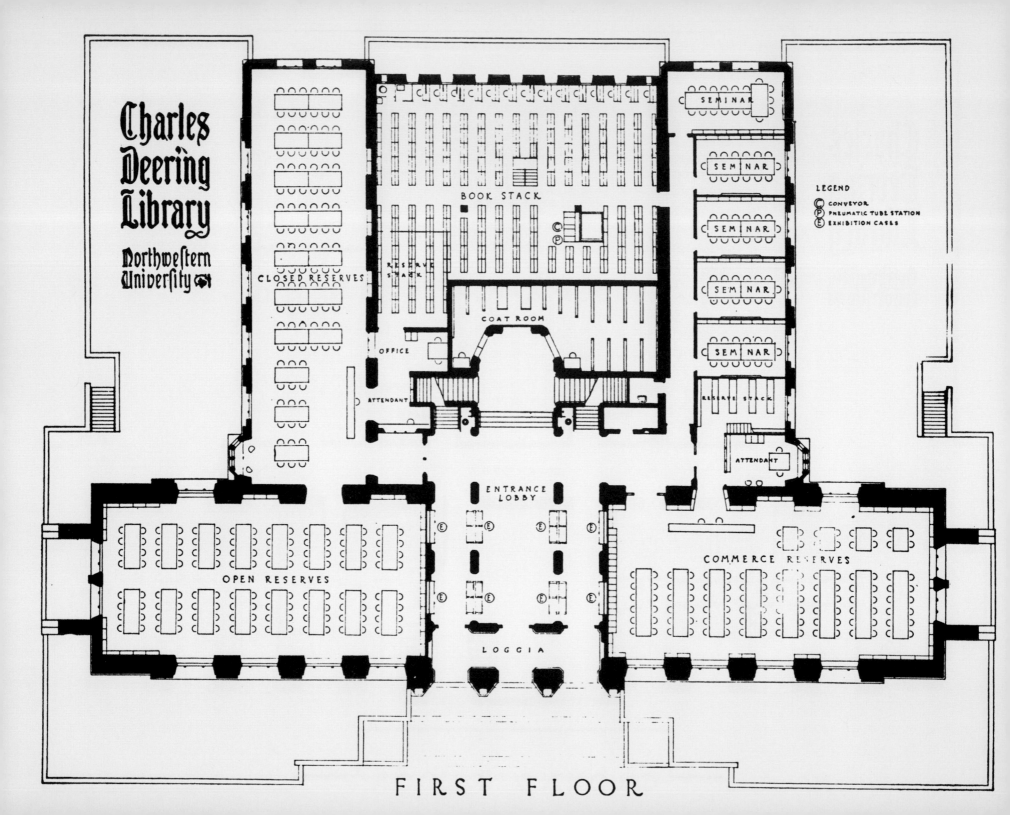

Charles
Deering
Library

Northwestern
University

CLOSED RESERVES

BOOK STACK

RESERVE STACK

COAT ROOM

OFFICE

ATTENDANT

SEMINAR

SEMINAR

SEMINAR

SEMINAR

SEMINAR

RESERVE STACK

ATTENDANT

LEGEND

Ⓒ CONVEYOR
Ⓟ PNEUMATIC TUBE STATION
Ⓔ EXHIBITION CASES

ENTRANCE
LOBBY

OPEN RESERVES

COMMERCE RESERVES

LOGGIA

FIRST FLOOR

A carving above the entrance from Deering Meadow proclaims, "The fountain of wisdom flows through books."

OPPOSITE: The legend for the first-floor plan specifies the locations of carrels, conveyor stations, and pneumatic tubes.

71

The main entrance lobby—
low ceilinged, beamed, stenciled,
decorated with carvings and
inscriptions—immediately evokes
a medieval feeling; exhibit cases
are original.

A phone booth—guarded,
appropriately, by a chattering
monkey—was cleverly designed to
suggest a confessional.

Stairway from the lobby to the
first floor

72

Painted stenciling, in the medieval style, decorates the intersections of the stone ceiling beams.

73

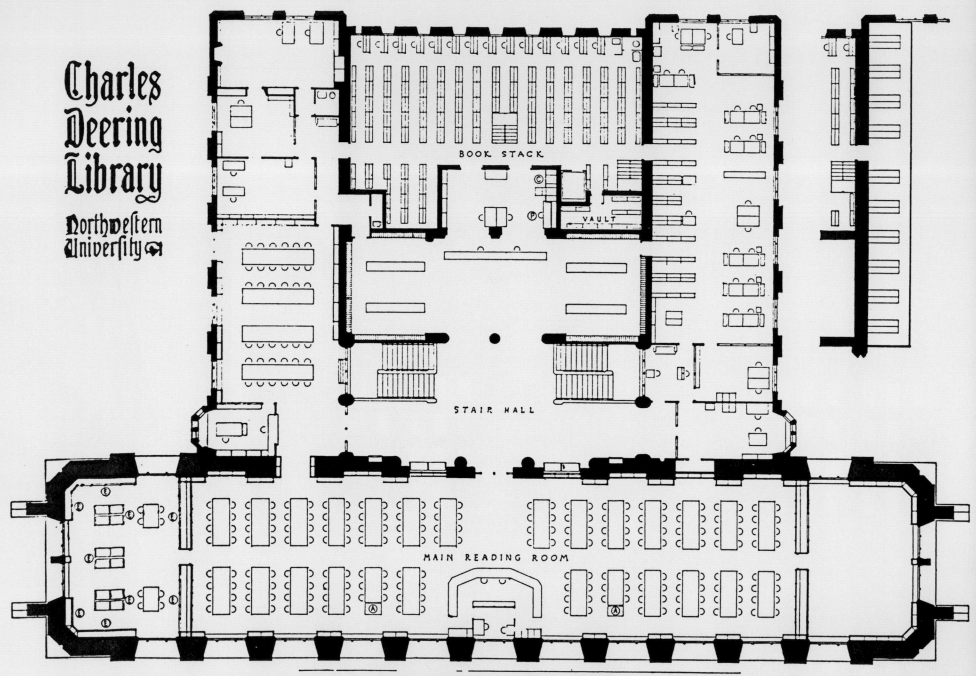

**Charles Deering Library**

**Northwestern University**

BOOK STACK

VAULT

STAIR HALL

MAIN READING ROOM

SECOND FLOOR

OPPOSITE: The inset at the right of the second-floor plan shows the extra gallery space above the librarians' workroom, which housed the massive Union Card Catalog.

The Deering Reading Room, circa 1949, with the original light fixtures

The Deering Reading Room today—
now the Art Collection

The original Browsing Room, where
Koch wanted students to be able to
indulge in leisure reading

The Circulation area, ready and waiting for the first student to check the card catalog and fill out a slip requesting a book from the closed stacks

The Union Card Catalog, in the mezzanine above the Cataloging Department, allowed librarians to locate books in libraries around the world.

On the north end of the space, the Rare Book Room, also known as the Treasure Room, housed the library's first editions, autographed copies, and antique volumes—a collection which Koch hoped to build upon.

Staff offices and workrooms were also located on the second floor. The cataloging room filled most of the south end, along with the order department and the assistant librarian's office. One of the innovations necessitated by the economic strictures on the size of the building was a mezzanine level, or gallery, over the cataloging workroom. This space held the Union Card Catalog, containing several million catalog cards issued by the Library of Congress and by other libraries, which allowed staff and researchers to find books not owned by Northwestern. On the north side of the building, east of the open-stack periodicals room, were the library administrative offices, including the university librarian's office in the northeast corner, with its mottoed fireplace and windows overlooking the lakeshore.

The rather austere basement level of Deering contained more seminar classrooms, a graduate reading room, shipping and receiving areas, newspaper and public documents stacks, and machine and service rooms. A luxurious multiroom staff lounge included a kitchen, resting room, showers, easy chairs, and refectory table. This level also gave access to the gardens—which Koch envisioned as outdoor reading rooms—on the north and south sides of the building.

Although the building was on three levels, there were six tiers of book stacks, with a capacity of 500,000 volumes (over 370,000 books were moved into the new Deering Library from Lunt). The building was designed to allow for easy future expansion upward and, most logically, eastward. It was anticipated that this expansion would be needed, and implemented, within a decade of the new library's opening.

Since the stacks were closed to undergraduates, the staff was kept busy filling readers' requests. State-of-the-art pneumatic tubes and conveyor belts moved call slips and books up and down the library's levels. Students found the title they needed in the card catalog, filled out call slips, and brought them to the circulation desk. A desk attendant removed the slips, sorted them by the stack level on which the book resided, and sent the slips by pneumatic tube to attendants stationed deep in the stacks, who located the books and put them on a conveyor belt that moved

The stacks

An intrepid Northwestern librarian uses a handy and ergonomic mechanism to update the card catalog.

A student stack assistant prepares to send a book up to the Circulation Desk.

Carrels, buried deep in the stacks, were havens for Northwestern scholars.

the books back up to the desk. The desk attendant called out the student's name, and the student could then check out the book.

The stacks areas included eighty-four carrels, each with writing surface, bookshelf, and chair, for the use of graduate students and faculty. As an article in the *Alumni News* pointed out, "These carrels are indeed a haven for students of all ages. . . . Here the solid provision of books within arm's reach offers the wealth of the past, while the lake shore, glimpsed through the windows, insists on the vigor of the present. The veriest dullard feels here that even he can achieve distinction, and the gifted one finds his capacities strengthened."

# LANDSCAPING THE GARDENS OF READING

The open space now known as Deering Meadow had played a colorful role in Northwestern's history. Originally called simply Campus Meadow, it served as the practice field for the newly organized football team from the 1880s until a field with grandstands was built on North Campus in 1891. From the nineteenth century, the meadow was the site of May Day (later May Week) events; originally a women's spring event marked by a dance around the eponymous pole, the festivities later became co-ed and included honors ceremonies and the May Sing. In addition to its role as a space for student relaxation and games, the Meadow was always used for concerts, speeches, and special events. To this day, although rumors occasionally surface that Deering Meadow is about to be built upon, or even under, Northwestern legend insists that the board of trustees will never allow this precious piece of open space—almost as symbolic as University Hall—to be destroyed.

Over the years, the meadow's shape was defined by a semicircle of buildings: Harris Hall, University Hall, Annie May Swift Hall, Heck Hall, and Memorial Hall. After Heck Hall burned in 1914, the center of the semicircle was empty until Deering Library took its place and gave the Meadow a new name. It also took on a new configuration.

The idea of "sloping lawns" surrounding the new library had been mentioned in the early planning stages, but Rogers's final drawings showed low, moated walls around the building's exterior, and a wide terrace in front. Rogers felt that the wall would draw attention to the entrance, and the terrace would help balance the two-hundred-foot length of the facade. But the terrace would also substantially decrease the size of the Meadow—and eliminate a number of old oak trees around the spot that would become the front entrance to Deering. In the summer of 1932, despite vociferous protests from faculty and students, more than a dozen oaks were cut down to allow the building of the terrace and steps.

Meanwhile, Koch pursued his search for a design for the new building's grounds. The extension of his vision for the new library to include the exterior surroundings

A May Day pageant on Campus Meadow, 1916 (University Hall and Annie May Swift in the background)

Barren of trees and landscaping, the new Deering Library stands between Deering Meadow and the lakeshore.

was not surprising from so detail-minded a man, and the landscaping plan took time to develop. Early in 1932, he invited a young landscape architect named Alfred Caldwell to suggest plans for the plantings and gardens. Caldwell (1903–98) was a protégé of Jens Jensen, one of the Midwest's best-known landscape architects and the designer of Northwestern's Shakespeare Garden. Caldwell's suggestions for Deering included circular pools in the north and south "moat" areas, and a wide path, to be called the Hawthorn Lane, leading to the lake—which, until the Lakefill project in the 1960s, was just a few yards from the library.

Reflecting Jensen's signature "Council Ring" formations, Caldwell envisioned a "Readers' Ring" by the lake where students could gather for classes or poetry readings. The Ring, Caldwell wrote, "is not a mere sentiment, it is as sane and staple as the potato." The ever-fanciful Koch loved the idea of a place for outdoor reading, but even he was realistic enough to recognize that the administration might consider it extravagant. He hoped that a future senior class would be inspired to present a Readers' Ring as its class gift.

Koch received Caldwell's recommendations and blueprint gratefully, but also asked for help—and comments on the Caldwell plan—from other sources. After hearing their criticism of the design, Koch's enthusiasm for Caldwell's ideas withered, and the landscaping of Deering proceeded without him. Caldwell went on to other commissions and to teach at the Illinois Institute of Technology, where he worked with Mies van der Rohe on the landscaping of that campus.

Northwestern's Building and Grounds Department submitted an alternative blueprint for the landscaping in October 1932, and planting began around the building and in the moatlike walled gardens. Trees, shrubs, and flowers included elm, plum, flowering crab, lilac, and dogwood trees, honeysuckle, roses, hydrangeas, mock orange, privet, forsythia, and 350 viburnum hedges.

Koch saw the sunken, walled gardens of the library as the perfect sites for open-air study spaces. He envisioned the garden on the north side as a forestlike environment, to be used in the fall while the weather was still warm. The south garden would be planted for use in the spring, with the walls deflecting chilly breezes. In addition to the plantings, he also gave thought to the furnishings—"metal chairs with spring seats and small circular tables with colorful umbrellas here and there for shade."

This 1939 photograph shows the original proximity of Deering (just to the right of the Meadow) to the lakeshore.

*From 1958 to 1962, among my most
favorite secret places—that no one
seemed to be aware of but me—were
the descended courtyards around
Deering. Spring and fall, they were so
welcoming, private, peaceful, beautiful,
well kept—with their benches and
solitude and butterflies and chipmunks
and squirrels. At that time you might
hear the lake—and most of your senses
could be caressed.*

LINDA MEEKS HARTFORD, CLASS OF 1962

The moat gardens in the 1940s

*I always loved exploring the statues in the grassy moat surrounding the library. We had to climb over the locked gates to get down the stairs into the area, which made it very exciting!*

KEN JONES, CLASS OF 1982

The moat gardens today

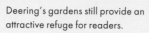

Deering's gardens still provide an attractive refuge for readers.

From left to right, T. W. Koch and Walter Dill Scott watch as H. G. Wells plants a tree outside the lower-level door on the south side of Deering, 1937. The tree is no longer there.

In the 1938 Northwestern summer school catalog, a paragraph on library holdings warned that, while students could take books outside, the library gardens were not "adjuncts of the bathing beaches, and are not to be used for 'sun baths' in bathing suits."

For the rest of his life, Koch continued to add plants that he obtained as gifts, or as transplants from the home gardens of Northwestern faculty and staff—leading him to refer to the library's "gardens of friendship." An arborvitae was planted outside the south Deering door by Koch and a notable visitor, H. G. Wells, in 1937. In September 1943, two years after Koch's death, the Deering Library's gardens were named the Koch Memorial Gardens, in honor of his devotion.

# GARDEN ART

In 1939 Koch was pleased to add a dramatic statue, a bronze Diana with her bow and hunting dog, to the north garden of the Deering Library. The Diana statue was a gift from its sculptor, Anna Hyatt Huntington (1876–1973). Huntington's teachers had included Hermon MacNeil, who created the pair of statues (locally known as "Pat" and "Jim") that guard Northwestern University's Patten Gym. Best known as a sculptor of animals, Huntington occasionally added a human figure (or, in this case, a goddess) to her sculptures. The Deering Diana was a replica of a statue Huntington created in 1922; at least seven other replicas stand in public and private sites in the United States and France. One of the numerous prizes Huntington won for her work was awarded for the Diana.

The acquisition of the Diana reflected Koch's remarkable ability to elicit gifts. Koch had contacted Huntington to ask about the wisdom of planting evergreens around garden statuary, and, he later wrote, "as a result of this correspondence, Mrs. Huntington became interested in my problem and presented to the Deering Library gardens a replica of her bronze statue of 'Diana.'" Koch later noted that the going rate for a Huntington Diana was $5,000.

By the time of Koch's death in 1941, several more sculptures had been added to the library gardens. Diana was joined in the north garden by a statue of the goddess Ceres, by Carl Heber. Koch had been attracted to the statue because it resembled Huntington's work. The west garden held a bronze David, by Paul Manship (gift of the Caxton Club, the organization for Chicago bibliophiles, of which Koch was a member). Both the Ceres and the David had been purchased from the estate of Charles M. Schwab in Pennsylvania. Ceres was a gift from Mrs. John Zane, widow of the Caxton Club president in whose memory Koch had planted nine evergreen trees in 1937, and the purchase of the David was eventually funded by the Caxton Club itself.

A marble fountain topped with a trio of bronze children (an anonymous gift to honor Koch), by Danish sculptor Rudolf Tegner, was placed in the south garden,

Anna Hyatt Huntington's Diana

David now stands guard over the
Art Collection reading room.

and *The Refugee*, a statuette by Jules L. Butensky (gift of Jacob Loeb) went into the southwest corner of the garden in 1942. The university donated a marble statue, *Two Children*. Eventually the Tegner, the Butensky, and the marble children were stolen, and after a vandalism incident the David was moved indoors to the lobby on the second floor of Deering, where he now keeps watch over the entrance to the Art Collection reading room. While Ceres continued to preside over the north garden, Diana was moved to the south garden in the 1980s.

*A treasure house of books indeed is the new Charles Deering Library, with its massive dignity, its delicate stone carvings, its vaulted aisles, its spacious rooms of books. Its impressive beauty commands the entire campus.*

ALUMNI NEWS, DECEMBER 1932

# The Moods of Deering Library

99

We were the first class to enjoy the extensive possibilities of NU's new library. It filled a great need in our educational development. As a day student, I spent many quiet, relaxed, and absorbing hours there. Besides, a rendezvous in the library was always a possibility. However, I'm sure I only scratched the surface of the library's riches . . .

MARY JO MILLER, CLASS OF 1933

*I think my library experience at Northwestern made me truly realize how much I love libraries. I am reminded of that* Twilight Zone *episode with Burgess Meredith as the book-obsessed bank worker who survived a nuclear holocaust by reading in the bank's vault. Deering was a home away from home for me while I was in attendance, and I will remember the hours, nay, the days I spent in research there fondly.*

ANTONIO JACOBS,
GRADUATE SCHOOL OF MUSIC, 2003

*I remember the feeling of awe the first time I went into Deering. It was then I realized I was at a serious institution of learning. The high ceilings, the long tables, and the sense that I was surrounded by knowledge remain with me today.*

JON PEVNA, CLASS OF 1967

# Chapter IV

# DEERING THROUGH THE DECADES

## 1933–2008

The construction of Deering Library took one and a half years, from the ground-breaking ceremony on June 14, 1931, when three generations of the Deering and McCormick families took a shovel to the soil, through the building, finishing, and moving process that culminated in December 1932. The final cost for the new building came to $1.25 million. The cubic footage was estimated at 1,43?,?1?3?, and square footage of the floor areas (including book stacks) at 90,117.

On December 29, 1932, during Northwestern's winter break, Charles Deering's two daughters cut the ceremonial ribbon across the main Reading Room doors, and his six grandchildren placed the first books on the shelves of Deering Library. President Scott led the dedication ceremony, declaring the library open, and symbolically charged out a book each to a Northwestern University student, an alumnus, a faculty member, and Roger McCormick. During a two-hour open house that evening, about three thousand visitors toured the new library.

The library officially opened on January 3, 1933, the first day of classes after winter break. Many years later, a Northwestern alumnus recalled his reaction on being the first student to use the new Charles Deering Library. He had arrived on campus early in the morning in order to complete an unfinished German assignment. He walked toward Lunt until he remembered that the new library would be open. Gathering the courage to push open the big wooden front door facing on to Deering Meadow, he entered the new building.

> There was complete silence. The only sound immediately thereafter were [sic] my own steps on the interior stone floor. To my right and left there appeared imposing double tiered stone staircases. I ascended the one to my right to the next floor. . . .

Members of the Deering, McCormick, and Danielson families cut the ribbon to open the Reading Room.

Janet Olson

Roger S. McCormick and his cousin Marion Danielson place the first books on the shelves of the new library during the dedication ceremony.

# Seduction and Ceremony

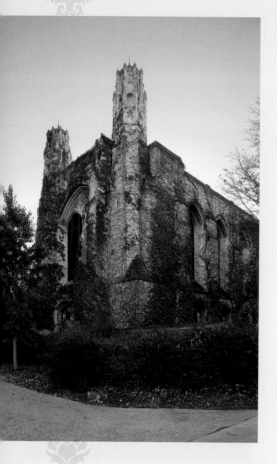

According to renowned architectural historian, critic, and Rogers scholar Aaron Betsky:

*The Charles Deering Library possesses a simple parti that exploits the simplicity of the design to maximum effect. The building presents itself as a simple box placed on top of a ridge overlooking a lawn [Deering Meadow]. The facade is divided into eleven equal bays by buttresses that start out as pronounced stone piers and at the top blend into the skin of the building. Each end elevation is organized around a single arched window, and the elaborately composed corners are held by piers topped by octagonal caps, which Rogers at one time had envisioned as towers. These corners act as clamps rising from the base to hold in place the top two floors, which appear as if they were a single volume held in a cage of stone piers. There is a delicate balance between the rigid march of the bays, grounded by the low arched windows and stone walls, and the ethereal quality of the reading room areas contained behind the glass windows, while the buttresses give one the sense that the whole box is riding the ridge.*

*The building then sets back a few times from the side elevation to contain what amounts to a second, rear, box whose facades are more closed and flat, since they contain little ornament or detail. This secondary set of shapes contain the bookstacks, expressed as a series of narrowly spaced stone sections facing what was then the rear of the campus, a marshy area next to Lake Michigan.*

*The front structure is in fact all that most visitors and users of the library inhabit, and within its shape a series of equally simple rectangular shapes are played off against a rich choreography meant, as at Yale, to slowly seduce one into the assimilation of knowledge through books. The visitor enters through one of three low arches—thus being confronted immediately with the structure of the building—then into a loggia of vaulted spaces covered with stone, much like a dark medieval crypt. Open reserve reading rooms occupy the ground floor on either side of this space, so that the casual user can avoid the ceremony of enlightenment promised by the strong sunshine washing down from the staircases immediately ahead.*

*The central axis disappears completely on the second floor. The building is here divided into a series of slots running at right angles to this axis and parallel to the ridge. The* "front of the house" *is taken up by a narrow* "Stair Hall," *which is nothing so much as a glorified double-loaded corridor through which one enters the two reading rooms on the sides and the main reading room in the center. The latter space is the main room of the building. It is an uninterrupted space of tall windows, long rows of desks [tables], and a high, wood-paneled [plaster] ceiling. Placed over the entrance and extending beyond the width of the other spaces, this room is the resting point at the end of the journey through the front part of the building. Along the way, hortatory inscriptions about the value of knowledge give one footnotes to the purpose of the journey, much in the way the decoration at Henri Labrouste's Bibliothèque Ste.- Geneviève illustrates a remarkably similar exposition of the parts of the reading library.* "No elaborate guide to the building nor direction signs will be needed," *explained librarian Theodore Koch;* "There is no danger of a freshman getting lost in a labyrinth of dark corridors."

From Aaron Betsky, *James Gamble Rogers and the Architecture of Pragmatism*, 1994. Reprinted by permission of The MIT Press.

An ornate set of double swinging doors in the center of the room caught my eye. I cautiously approached them, opened one of them, and after taking a peek I stepped cautiously into what appeared to be the center of some kind of vaulted cathedral with a lengthy double series of long well-lighted tables and arm chairs instead of pews to the right and to the left. Yes, even many shelves of books added to the splendor! . . .

I seated myself at one of the library tables to the left to begin my studies but I never did complete the German assignment that day. For the next hour I watched members of the student body as they entered the reading room through those same swinging doors. I wish I could have made camera recordings of the variety of their expressions of awe as they first witnessed the magnificence of this new educational environment.

Other visitors were equally awed. A librarian from England, touring various libraries on her way to and from the Century of Progress World's Fair in Chicago in 1933, wrote that

> one of the finest of all libraries must surely be the Charles Deering Library at Northwestern University outside Chicago, combining as it does the beauty of age with absolute newness and every modern equipment and possessing an excellent collection of books. . . . The Reading Room has a mellowness that belies its age, with its solid, refectory like tables, and beautifully carved wooden screen, on which are many quaint carvings of animals and birds. . . . The staff are fortunate in having a large room for meetings or meals, a luxuriously appointed kitchen, and even a bedroom.

On the other hand, a gleefully embellished legend still popular among Northwestern alumni says that architect Frank Lloyd Wright compared the new library to a pig (alternatively, a sow) lying on its back. Its most developed version has Walter Dill Scott inviting Frank Lloyd Wright to christen the building in 1933. After cutting the ribbon, Wright turns to Scott and says, "You have built the ugliest structure I have ever seen. It looks not like a library, but like a rotisserie pig broiling over an open pit; the four Gothic towers are its stubby legs jutting into the sky." In dismay, Scott decrees that the front doors of Deering Library are to remain closed and locked forever. The story is apocryphal, and its origins are unclear. Wright was not at the ribbon cutting, and Deering's front doors remained in use from the morning the building opened until after the Main Library debuted in the 1970s.

THE BOARD OF TRUSTEES
THE PRESIDENT
AND THE FACULTIES OF
NORTHWESTERN UNIVERSITY
REQUEST THE HONOR OF
YOUR PRESENCE
AT THE DEDICATION OF
THE CHARLES DEERING LIBRARY
THURSDAY AFTERNOON
DECEMBER TWENTY-NINTH
NINETEEN THIRTY-TWO
AT FIVE O'CLOCK
EVANSTON, ILLINOIS

Invitation to the dedication of the new Charles Deering Memorial Library, December 29, 1932

Circulation Desk, circa 1948

Students in the Browsing Room,
circa 1948

# BETWEEN THE DEPRESSION AND WORLD WAR II

When it opened, Deering Library contained close to four hundred thousand volumes (including pamphlets). In addition to Deering, separate libraries on the Evanston campus served the School of Music and the departments of astronomy, chemistry, geology, and botany. The thirty-four library staff members were assisted by thirty or forty students receiving government aid. The university had been a government depository since 1876, receiving materials distributed by the U.S. Government Printing Office, but now there was space in the new library for a separate government documents room, and a specialized librarian was hired for the department.

Areas of the new library were quickly adapted for unanticipated uses. Koch noted students' tendency to use Deering as their "headquarters throughout the day," congregating in the lower level to smoke and talk. He considered turning a seminar space into a smoking room, but hesitated to lose another classroom. Seminar 109 had already become a typing room where students could bring their own typewriters and copy out the material they needed from books that could not leave the library.

Throughout the years of Depression belt-tightening, Koch kept up his demands on behalf of the library. While the Deering and McCormick families' gifts had provided most of the funds for the building's construction, there was no endowment for maintenance, collections, or staffing. With the space problem solved (for the moment), Koch continued to lobby for money for books and salaries. In 1936 he noted that the book fund was $14,000 lower than it had been the year the library moved from Lunt. Salaries had been cut 19 percent, and there was a serious staff turnover problem: fourteen assistants had resigned because of low wages.

In 1939, Walter Dill Scott retired from the presidency of the university. Scott's contribution to Northwestern was celebrated at the dedication, in 1940, of Scott Hall, the long-needed student center—designed by James Gamble Rogers. With its meeting rooms, lounges, and basement, Scott Hall relieved some of the pressure on Deering Library to serve as a gathering space, especially for the many commuter and part-time students. Funding for Scott Hall came from the contributions of more than eleven thousand individuals and organizations, including money raised from the sale of snacks dubbed "Scottwiches."

Students in the Browsing Room, circa 1948

Main Reading Room, circa 1948

*My instant memory of Deering is of the stomachaches I used to get because I only went to Deering to study for midterms and finals. After I calmed down, though, I felt that studying at Deering was the epitome of sophistication!*

LINDA BECKER SALTZMAN,
CLASS OF 1967

Circa 1948

# WORLD WAR II AND THE POSTWAR YEARS

he new president of the university was Franklyn Bliss Snyder (1884–1958), who had begun his career at Northwestern in 1909 as a faculty member in the English Department. President Snyder was immediately faced with the problems of preparing the university for the war effort, which required new uses of space across the campus. Although the number of male students decreased during the war, the male population of the university was increased by nearly fifty thousand trainees attending the Reserve Midshipmen's School, Navy V-12, Radio School, Army Medical and Dental School, and other military training programs on the Evanston and Chicago campuses. Later in the war years, discharged veterans—older than most undergraduates—began arriving to complete or begin their college educations. Faculty and staff, however, were in short supply, as four hundred faculty members joined the military service, and others worked on Northwestern's eighty-seven research contracts with the U.S. government. The functions of many buildings were adapted to wartime needs, while student housing, already a problem before the war, became a crisis.

In the library, an era ended when T. W. Koch died unexpectedly on March 23, 1941, after twenty-two years as university librarian. President Snyder's memorial address described Koch's "contagious devotion to scholarship" and his "rich human personality," with its appealing "childlikeness," but also described him as "a magnificent fighter for the things in which he believed." Koch was temporarily replaced by assistant librarian Effie Keith, who assumed the post of acting university librarian until a new university librarian was hired in 1944.

Meanwhile, the war affected all aspects of library operations, from acquisitions to space usage to staffing. Materials published in Axis-controlled countries were detained in Bermuda before being released to American libraries, and some items ordered from England were "lost at sea through enemy action." Keith used funds normally allocated for European publications—now unavailable—to expand the library's North and South American holdings. However, other budget cuts forced students to borrow required books from the Evanston Public Library. Library staff moved the business books out of the Commerce Reading Room and turned the room over to the Naval V-12 program.

Effie Keith (1882–1969), whose service to the university library spanned half a century, from 1916 to 1966, was acting university librarian from 1941 to 1944.

Franklyn Bliss Snyder (1884–1958) was Northwestern's president from 1939 to 1949.

While the number of male civilian students declined during World War II, the campus saw a huge influx of military trainees.

Nearly 150 temporary structures—
Quonset and Steelcraft huts—were
installed from South Campus to
Dyche Stadium to house the great
numbers of returning veterans
(many of whom brought their
wives and children). Some of the
huts remained in use as classroom
buildings until the mid-1950s.

116

Deering Library was part of my "real estate" when I lived in the Lunt Quonset Huts at Foster and Sheridan as a freshman in 1951 to 1952. As I looked eastward across the meadow each morning, Deering was like a beautiful Tudor castle. It was given a musical identity during summer evening concerts by the university concert band, and I fondly remember retired, longtime band director Glen Cliff Bainum leaning on one of the audience bleachers, nodding his approval of the music directed by his successor, John Paynter.

GEORGE BERES, CLASS OF 1955

Chicago-area universities circulated bulletins outlining the steps to preserve each institution's most valuable records and materials in case of an air raid; fortunately, the move of physics, chemistry, and engineering books to the new Technological Institute Library, early in 1942, had freed up space in Deering that could be used for emergency storage of Northwestern's treasures.

With the war came new demands on library staff. Tech librarian Hazel Walz was told to remove books relating to explosives, torpedoes, and structural defense from the shelves, and to "take the names and addresses of all persons requesting such material." The Military Intelligence Division of the War Department asked the library for a list of all its Japanese books, maps, and photos. Reference librarians compiled numerous specialized bibliographies to answer questions focused on war topics. Meanwhile, materials (many of them restricted) flowed into the Government Documents Department, designated a War Key Information Center. The extra work was accomplished in spite of salary cuts, staff shortages, and high turnover. Twenty people—half the staff, including the new tech librarian and the documents librarian—left to join the war effort during the 1942–43 academic year.

Keith kept the library functioning as normally as possible. She insisted on the library's responsibility for "keeping alive the interest in literature and the arts, in spite of the present necessary emphasis on science and technology." President Snyder agreed, stressing the enduring importance of a liberal arts education and asserting that "the only worthy physical symbol on our campus of Northwestern's faith in the humanities and social sciences is Deering Library."

In 1944, Jens Nyholm was named university librarian, a position he held until 1968. (Effie Keith resumed her previous title of assistant librarian.) He saw the university slowly recover from the effects of the war, facing tight budgets, an influx of students, and an increasingly crowded library. While Rogers, Scott, and Koch had incorporated ease of expansion into Deering's design, their plans for the future, conceived during the height of the Depression, were predicated on the return of prosperity. Then the war created a shortage of materials and labor, and building projects were not a priority for the university—only two buildings had gone up since 1941. During the postwar years, the university's income and staffing remained depleted, while at the same time the student population increased dramatically, from about 4,800 in 1943–44 to 9,600 in 1948–49, as veterans—many of them benefiting from the G.I. Bill—resumed or began their education.

Jens Nyholm (1900–1983), Northwestern's university librarian from 1944 to 1968

# THE FABULOUS FIFTIES

ut significant changes were about to take place throughout the university, driven by the dynamic personality of J. Roscoe—"Rocky"—Miller, who became president of Northwestern in 1949. Miller focused on raising the quality of the Northwestern University faculty, a goal that depended on improving the physical facilities on both campuses. The success of fund-raising efforts associated with the 1950–51 Centennial Celebration enabled him to move ahead with his plans. Between 1952 and 1955, eight buildings went up, including one academic building (Kresge Centennial Hall), three dormitories, and the McGaw Memorial Hall sports facility and auditorium.

Northwestern's 1953–54 catalog boasted that the university's land and buildings were worth $34,000,000. Full-time students on the Evanston campus numbered around 6,400, served by 1,050 faculty members. Base tuition was $200 per quarter, with room and board ranging between $500 and $900 per year.

In 1950, the millionth volume was added to the library's collection. A gala ceremony to mark the occasion was held on July 26, 1950, in the Commerce Reading Room. Although university librarian Nyholm had originally suggested a presentation Bible as a suitable millionth book, the volume that was chosen to mark the occasion was a vellum-bound incunabulum of the *Didascalicon* (Book of Knowledge), written in the twelfth century by French monk and mystic Hugh St.Victor (1096–1141) and printed in Strasbourg around 1475. (The *Didascalicon* is still located in Deering, in the McCormick Library of Special Collections.)

Thirty-year-old Roger S. McCormick, the grandson of Charles Deering, presented the millionth volume on behalf of his parents, Chauncey and Marion Deering McCormick. By now McCormick was an old hand at Deering Library traditions; at the age of twelve he had laid the library's cornerstone and at thirteen placed the first book on its shelves. Trustee Kenneth Burgess accepted the McCormicks' gift, and Nyholm affixed a special bookplate that read, "This is the millionth volume in Northwestern University Libraries. . . . Presented by Mr. and Mrs. Chauncey McCormick, July 26, 1950." Also participating in the ceremony were representatives from Northwestern's Chicago campus schools—dental, law, medical, and University College, each presenting a volume on

J. Roscoe Miller (1905–1977) became president of the university in 1949, after serving as Medical School dean. He oversaw a massive building campaign throughout the university.

When I was a student in the early 1980s, J. D. Salinger was my absolute idol (imagine embarrassingly immense hero worship on a movie star level!), and when I discovered that Northwestern had a rare copy of his unauthorized collection of short stories in Special Collections in Deering and that I, a lowly undergraduate student, could just go and look at it, hold it, and read it . . . well, all the tuition money my parents had forked over seemed well spent. I almost cried when I held that fragile little book in my hands.

LESLIE PIETRZYK, CLASS OF 1983

121

Roger S. McCormick (second from left), who as a boy had laid the library's cornerstone, places the millionth volume on the shelf on July 26, 1950, assisted by (left to right) board of trustees president Kenneth Burgess, President Miller, and university librarian Nyholm.

behalf of a donor to that school's library. In his speech, Nyholm predicted that two million volumes would meet Northwestern's future academic needs.

On a number of counts, 1951 was a landmark year at Northwestern University. It marked the university's centennial, an occasion for revisiting the past and launching building campaigns for the future. The library took a less spectacular but surprisingly important step forward that year by opening the formerly closed stacks to all students. Open stacks were still a rarity in academic libraries at that time—only two or three other institutions preceded Northwestern in making this change. The new approach gave students direct access to the library's holdings, allowing them to browse the shelves rather than submitting call slips and waiting for books. Another

In 1951, the university marked its centennial on Deering Meadow.

very significant consideration was that eliminating the paging system resulted in a welcome reduction in the library's operating costs.

Nyholm noted that opening the stacks was undertaken cautiously, following "evolutionary rather than revolutionary principles": stacks were opened to seniors in January 1950, and to juniors in September of that year. An experimental open-to-all program was implemented during the 1951 summer session. Despite fears that students might misshelve the books they retrieved and that the stacks might become noisy, disturbing the users of the carrels in those areas, the new system was maintained and the pneumatic tubes, conveyor belts, and library assistants stationed in the stacks awaiting call slips became things of the past.

Registration, 1947

Registration, 1967

*When I think of Deering, I think of two things: 1) registration and the long lines in the foyer; and 2) the stacks—and the activities that took place there (or so we heard!!!).*

JOAN EHRLICH, CLASS OF 1967

Nyholm may not have realized that opening the stacks would indeed have a revolutionary impact: open stacks changed the nature of the relationship between students and books and would open the door to new concepts in library design that replaced large, common reading rooms with individual or small-group study areas in or near the book stacks.

In the summer of 1954, Deering Library played a starring role during the Second Assembly of the World Council of Churches, a conference that brought more than 1,200 international visitors to Evanston. The entire event received considerable press coverage nationwide, especially on August 19, when U.S. president Dwight D. Eisenhower attended the conference. Along with a number of important World Council of Churches delegates, presidents Eisenhower and Miller assembled in Deering's entrance lobby; the processional filed through the great arched doorway onto Deering Meadow, where Eisenhower delivered a special convocation address and received an honorary Doctor of Laws degree.

Also in 1954, Jens Nyholm was completing his first decade as head librarian. He continued to hope, just as his predecessors had done, for more space and more staff. The library was overcrowded, its shelves and reading rooms filled well beyond their intended capacity with books and patrons. And, in the past five years, the number of staff members had fallen by seventeen. According to the annual Association of Research Libraries statistics, Northwestern University Library, with 1,446,163 volumes (nearly three times the capacity Deering had been designed to hold) and ninety-eight on staff, was lagging behind its peer institutions in funding and services.

Nyholm and his staff continued to find creative solutions to the library's storage problems—including housing portions of the collection in the basements under the Dearborn Observatory and Harris Hall. Nyholm played an instrumental role in forming the Midwest Inter-Library Center (later renamed the Center for Research Libraries)—a cooperative storage and distribution center for infrequently used books from several institutions' collections—that could store nearly eighty tons of Northwestern's books. As the space problem persisted, the

U.S. president Dwight D. Eisenhower (fifth from left) proceeds down the steps of Deering with university president Miller during the World Council of Churches meeting, August 19, 1954.

*Northwestern Library News* reported that "between quarters the 'Deering shift' was in operation again."

> "Deering shift" is a bibliographic rather than a football term, and refers to the movement of books within and out of our crowded book stacks. This time the history collections were extended into the east wing of the gallery [stacks]. . . . This move completes the internal expansion possible within Deering's walls without intruding book shelves into communications and lobby areas.

Then another temporary solution to Deering's book-storage problem was found. The Chicago *Sun-Times* reported in October 1955 that books were on the move at Northwestern, headed for an innovative new facility located underground. The subterranean space was formed from the basement that remained after Fayerweather Hall (built in 1886 and used as a science building until 1942) was torn down in 1954. Enlarged to about an acre of storage space, and extending under the landscaped grounds of brand-new Kresge Centennial Hall, the new storage vault cost over $290,000 to build. Along with space for the library, the facility would store the School of Speech's theater props, the geology department's rock collection, and Building and Grounds equipment.

Student workers assembled the new, freestanding industrial shelving for the "Library Annex," and librarians collected faculty-approved books for off-site storage. The move had to be postponed when test volumes developed mildew, but once the humidity was adjusted, the Annex provided twenty thousand square feet of space for about two hundred thousand volumes. Soon the Library Annex was old news, although the *Daily Northwestern* ran occasional articles with such headlines as "Not All 'Above Board' at NU" and "Big Vault Is Mystery to Frosh."

As the years passed, more books were added to the Annex, but it was always seen as a temporary solution; only an extensive renovation and addition to the library building would solve the problem. In 1957, the architectural firm Holabird & Root & Burgee drew up plans for a proposed expansion to Deering. The sketch shows a north/south rectangular structure added to the stacks section, creating an H-shaped building—not unlike the double-E shape of Holabird & Root's 1942 Technological Institute—but no steps were taken toward building the addition.

# NORTHWESTERN UNIVERSITY
# OUTGROWS ITS LIBRARY—AGAIN

As the 1960s began, the use of space within Deering had been adjusted somewhat from the original 1930s plans. Instead of a typing room, students now had access to a copy center which had been added to the first level, behind the stairs leading to the second level. The first level still held two general reserve reading rooms and the School of Business reading room (its name was changed from Commerce Reading Room in 1953). On the second level, the space on the south end of the reading room that Koch had lovingly called the Browsing Room had become part of Special Collections. Additional Special Collections holdings were located in a former men's lounge on the ground floor. Former ground-floor seminar rooms now held the African Library, the Curriculum Library (for the School of Education, including a collection of children's literature), and the University Archives, which had been established in Deering in 1935.

In 1960 a student lounge was formally installed on the ground-floor corridor. This long-sought innovation was the result of a persistent campaign mounted by one Rich Gephardt, a School of Speech student and a member of the student government organization. The lounge was equipped with telephones, smoking facilities, and tables where students could use their portable typewriters. When Gephardt became president of the Student Senate the next year, Nyholm wrote to express his pleasure that the Senate would be led by "a man who understands the importance of the library as well as its problems." (Gephardt later distinguished himself in politics beyond the Student Senate.) Six walnut benches, originally in the old U.S. Court House in Chicago, were added to the lobby lounge a few years later.

In addition to the collections in Deering, eight branch libraries continued to serve their niche audiences on the Evanston campus. Nyholm had centralized their administration, but the collections themselves remained scattered. Branch libraries included the Music Library, located in the Music Administration building; the Transportation Library, in the Transportation Center at 1810 Hinman; and the Map Library, in University Hall.

# THE "MONSTER ON THE KNOLL"

I t was common knowledge on campus that the library had needed an extension since the mid-1940s, and articles in the *Daily Northwestern* expressed sympathy for the librarians' plight and the lack of funds for making changes. And they continued to voice criticism of the lighting, heating, and noise in the library. To one student writing in a 1960 issue of the *Daily*'s weekly magazine *Dimension*, Koch's Gothic dream had become "the Monster on the Knoll," a "pseudo-Gothic cavern of lost books, poor lighting, uncontrollable heating and six indoor outhouses [that] has waged unrelenting warfare against Northwestern's students, faculty, administration, and librarians. . . ." The building itself was something "no sane person would build today."

> The Monster's creators endowed it with millions of cubic feet of space, but precious little which could be allocated for the storage of books. . . . They gave the Monster windows worthy of a cathedral (for which no suitable drapes could be found until last year). . . . The students using Deering have also encountered the ingenious devices contrived by the builders to make human life unbearable. The main reading room is lighted by a number of lamps which gently swing back and forth while one is trying to read. . . . The lighting in stacks seems calculated to leave one blind within four years. . . . The students, alternately sweltering and shivering, grope through the library's eternal twilight. . . . Deering has the acoustics of a prosperous boiler plant—and hundreds of students holding impromptu political debates, fraternity meetings, social exchanges, and pre-examination seminars compound the chaos.

It was obvious that a building constructed in 1932 for five hundred thousand books in closed stacks to serve a student population of five thousand could not be expected to hold over a million books and meet the needs of over eight thousand students.

# A NEW UNIVERSITY LIBRARY

inally, in 1961, a new library building was proposed as a part of a building program based on pushing the campus eastward onto lakefill. University president Miller appointed a Library Planning and Building Committee, chaired by history professor Clarence Ver Steeg. With extensive input from members of the university community, and working closely with architect Walter Netsch of Skidmore, Owings and Merrill, the committee oversaw the creation of the new building.

The new library had as much vision, theory, and passion behind its planning as had gone into Deering, with a result totally different—reflecting the aesthetic of the times, advances in technology, and new interpretations of the purpose of a library. Deering Library represented the age of closed stacks and large central reading rooms, echoing a library tradition that went back to monastic and early university libraries. The new library would be firmly situated in the age of open stacks, with reading areas of all sizes positioned throughout the space. Architect Netsch, as well known for his designs as James Gamble Rogers had been in his day, envisioned the library as a space divided according to academic fields of study into sections (towers) that were connected by links. Had Koch imagined that research libraries could be open for browsing, he might well have agreed with the concept that Netsch described:

> An important way to relate the individual to subject materials is to articulate the research collection into reader-book pavilions. The radial system permits the search of 125,000 volumes from a single vantage point, and the extension of the perimeter accommodates areas of varying sizes for seminar rooms, faculty studies, carrels, and typing rooms. The repetitive pattern of the research portions of the tower pavilions expresses a different reader-book relationship.

Groundbreaking for the new university library took place in 1966, and the building—a three-towered structure with a broad plaza—was completed in 1969. The

Architect Walter Netsch, of Skidmore, Owings and Merrill, worked with Ver Steeg and the Library Committee to create a building that met contemporary needs.

The link between old and new

History professor Clarence Ver Steeg (1922–2007), chair of the Library Planning and Building Committee, in front of the brand-new university library, 1970.

new library was attached to Deering by a corridor that joined the new main floor to the old ground floor, and by a link on the third level. Construction costs came to $12,321,906, or $31 per square foot, with 330,000 square feet of assignable space—enough room to hold 1.5 million volumes, with seating for almost one thousand people. Like Deering in 1933, the new university library also was meant to be expandable once its capacity was reached, by the simple addition of a fourth tower.

The task of moving into the new building involved transferring and merging volumes from Deering's stacks. On December 1, 1969, a few collections from Deering were moved to the new library without disruption of service, but the main parts of the move occurred between December 18 and January 19, 1970. The library closed, circulation of books ceased, and all services were suspended as the books were moved and placed on the shelves in the new towers. The dedication of the new Northwestern University Library took place on the Library Plaza on the afternoon of October 21, 1970.

# DEERING IN THE MAIN LIBRARY ERA

fter 1970, Deering was no longer the university library, but took on a new role as the site of specialized libraries and collections. The collections remaining in Deering—including the University Archives, Special Collections, the Management Library, and Government Documents—were gradually relocated in expanded quarters, and new collections were added. However, the African Library moved out of Deering to its new home in the east tower of the new building (the collection, usually referred to as Africana, was renamed the Melville J. Herskovits Library of African Studies that same year).

The Transportation Library moved from 1810 Hinman to the top floor of Deering in 1972, occupying the space along the north side of the building formerly occupied by the librarians' workrooms. (Transportation relocated again, into the university library, in 1983.) At the same time, Special Collections moved into its present location, in the former area of the administrative offices and periodicals room. The former grand Reading and Reference Room became the Art Library.

On the ground floor, the University Archives expanded into additional rooms, and Government Publications moved from the north side to the south side of the building. To accommodate students in the Graduate School of Management, a tunnel was built to connect Leverone Hall with Deering, permitting easy access to the Management Collection and the Main Library. In 1976, the Music Library moved into the second floor (formerly the main level) of Deering. This was the Music Library's third move; after outgrowing its original home in the Music Administration building, it occupied a temporary location at 1810 Hinman before making its permanent home in Deering.

With Deering's collections settled into their new locations, the need to promote and secure them became clear, along with the larger issue of the building's overall

Deering Library's fiftieth-anniversary celebration, November 1982

Charles Deering McCormick (right) and his son, Hilleary, shelve the three-millionth volume in 1983.

condition. On November 10, 1982, the organization of donors then known as the Library Council held a celebration to commemorate Deering Library's fiftieth anniversary. An exhibit in the lobby depicted the planning and construction of the building, and members of the Deering and McCormick families were in attendance. Northwestern president Robert Strotz used the occasion to launch the Deering Library Preservation Project, a $1.5 million campaign to relieve overcrowding in the library's stacks, enhance exhibit facilities, improve security, and install modern environmental controls to replace the now-antiquated heating and ventilation system in the building. The project was completed in 1986, and celebrated by a Library Council Gala at which Scott Bennett, assistant university librarian for collection management, noted, "We have transformed the conditions in which [the] wealth of research material in Deering Library are held. But we have not transformed Deering Library."

As the Deering Preservation Project proceeded, a ceremony marking the library's acquisition of its three-millionth volume on September 19, 1983, echoed the events of thirty-three years earlier. Charles Deering McCormick, accompanied by his son, Hilleary McCormick, presented and shelved the volume in Deering Library. This time, the book was a more modern one—although the text was not: *The Four Gospels* (Golden Cockerel Press, 1931), with typeface and woodcuts by twentieth-century designer Eric Gill. This book is also housed in Deering Library's Department of Special Collections.

The Deering family continued its philanthropy to the university library, largely as a result of the continuing interests of Charles Deering McCormick (1915–94), Charles Deering's grandson. In 1970, he and his brothers contributed the funds for the construction of the south tower. He and his wife, Nancy, also gave gifts to endow the position of university librarian and to create an endowment in memory of their son, Hilleary, who died in 1985, to support the humanities collections. Following her husband's death in 1994, Nancy McCormick made substantial gifts to endow and name the Charles Deering McCormick Library of Special Collections in memory of her husband.

Charles Deering McCormick and nephew Peter McCormick enjoy an exhibit commemorating the construction of Deering Library during the fiftieth-anniversary celebration.

The Deering Library Preservation Project funded much-needed interior and structural renovation work. The project was completed in 1986.

## ERICKSON GARDEN

The library gardens had become neglected during the decades after T. W. Koch's death. In the 1980s, after doing research in Koch's papers, Circulation Services head Rolf Erickson, a gardening enthusiast, worked with R. Russell Maylone of Special Collections and Patrick Quinn of the University Archives to plan a restoration of the Koch Memorial Gardens. The university's landscape architect drew up plans in 1988, but Erickson died in 1992, before the restoration plan could be funded. Fund-raising began in 1993 to carry through with the garden plan. Work finally began in 1996, and included planting flowers, shrubs, and ornamental grasses, and the installation of wooden benches, to create the atmosphere of an English cottage garden. The restored Erickson-Koch Garden on the south side of Deering Library was dedicated on October 6, 2001.

# DEERING LIBRARY TODAY

oday Deering Library is firmly entrenched as a symbol of the university. As photogenic and easily recognized as University Hall (1869), the building appears frequently on university greeting cards and promotional materials.

Nearly nineteen generations of students have passed through its doors. Alums who had complained about the crowded shelves and bad lighting during their student days now return to Deering with warm memories, noting with nostalgic fondness the worn steps leading up to the second floor and enjoying the glow of afternoon light through the stained-glass medallions. Today's students are impressed by the Gothic spaces, which remind them of Harry Potter's Hogwarts.

Like the Gothic cathedrals that were its inspiration, Deering was built to last forever—a fitting setting for the collections of special distinction that are housed within its walls. To librarian Koch, Deering Library was a "shrine for books;" to President Snyder, a "worthy physical symbol of Northwestern's faith in the humanities and social sciences." President Bienen characterizes it as an "intellectual heirloom" of the university.

Perhaps the reminiscence of an alumnus best captures the role of Deering as a symbol, an educational center, and a place for students at Northwestern University. "When I think of Northwestern, I think of Deering," wrote Wallace Mlyniec (class of 1967). "Deering was magnificent. You could not enter without knowing you were in a university. It soared, it inspired, it created dreams, and made one want to succeed. It was also a great place to find a date."

# THE ART COLLECTION

Northwestern University Library's Art Collection houses 150,000 cataloged volumes and subscribes to five hundred journals and twenty major databases in art, architecture, design, photography, and related visual arts. The collection supports the research and curricular needs of Art History, Art Theory and Practice, and other arts and humanities departments at the university, and is especially strong in nineteenth- and twentieth-century Western art and architectural serials. In addition to the Reading Room, the Art Collection in recent years has expanded into an adjacent Architecture Reading Room and has opened an Art Research Center for faculty and graduate students.

Housed in Deering's most fondly remembered room—the onetime main Reading Room—the Art Collection also hosts some of the library's most treasured works of art, and those most associated with its namesake family. Portraits of William Deering, Charles Deering, Marion Whipple Deering, James Deering, and Roger Deering hang on its walls. It is also home to a famous portrait of the French avant-garde composer Erik Satie, *Erik Satie, El Bohemio*, by the Catalan painter Ramon Casas. Casas was a friend of Charles Deering, who met him while studying painting in Paris in the early 1890s. The portrait was bequeathed to the library by Deering's daughter, Marion Deering McCormick, in 1956, and has in recent years traveled to exhibitions at the Metropolitan Museum of Art in New York and the National Gallery of Art in Washington, D.C. More information about the Art Collection and its holdings and services can be found online at www.library.northwestern.edu/art.

*Erik Satie, El Bohemio*, 1891, by Ramon Casas

Marion Whipple Deering (1857–1943), wife of Charles Deering;
portrait by Wayman Adams

Roger Deering (1884–1936), son of Charles Deering;
portrait by Wayman Adams

# GOV INFO

Willem Janszoon Blaeu's 1635 map of Africa, "Africa nova description," from GovInfo's collection of antique African maps

The Government and Geographic Information and Data Services department, informally known as GovInfo, is one of the oldest and largest designated U.S. government document depositories in the nation. Established in 1876, its collection includes government materials dating as far back as the late 1700s and as up-to-the-minute as a database that lets researchers map certain kinds of data by location, allowing them to discover trends not readily revealed by spreadsheets or statistical tables. Its federal, state, and local records include congressional hearings and reports; presidential papers; publications by all federal agencies; and documents from Cook County, Chicago, and Evanston. It also functions as an official depository for several international organizations, including the United Nations, the European Union, and the World Tourism Organization. The more than 200,000 maps in its extensive Map Collection range from the local to the international—from the first map of Illinois, commissioned in 1818 shortly before it was granted statehood (which places the long-abandoned town of Kaskaskia as its capital), to a collection of antique African maps dating as far back as 1530, which received worldwide media attention when it was digitized and launched online in 2007 (www.library .northwestern.edu/govinfo/collections/ mapsofafrica). As a government document depository, GovInfo is open to and serves the general public as well as the Northwestern community. More information on its resources and services can be found online at www .library.northwestern.edu/govinfo.

# McCORMICK LIBRARY OF SPECIAL COLLECTIONS

Now headquartered in what was originally Deering's Periodicals Room, Special Collections houses more than 225,000 of Northwestern University Library's most unusual, unique, and valuable items. Besides books, manuscripts, and periodicals, the collection also contains sound recordings, photographs, posters, and prints—ranging across history from a set of 3,500-year-old Mesopotamian tablets to the most recent issues of contemporary feminist journals from around the world. Among its many treasures: the only sketch James Joyce is ever known to have made of *Ulysses* protagonist Leopold Bloom, and a diary page on which D. H. Lawrence recorded the list of famous literary friends who'd sent him checks to pay for copies of his newly self-published novel, *Lady Chatterley's Lover*. In recent years, Special Collections has worked with collaborators inside and outside the library to digitize selected collections, making them freely accessible to researchers around the globe. As a result, for example, Native American tribes across North America have discovered portraits of their ancestors in

Edward S. Curtis's *The North American Indian* collection and requested use of the images for documentaries, educational videos, and other projects aimed at reconstructing their lost histories. Information regarding many of the resources and services of the McCormick Library of Special Collections is available online at www .library. northwestern.edu/spec.

Mesopotamian cuneiform tablets

James Joyce's sketch of Leopold Bloom

# THE MUSIC LIBRARY

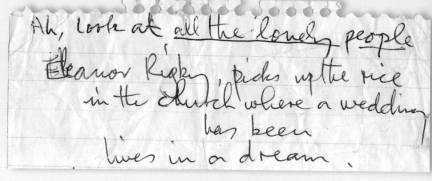

Original notes for the lyrics to the Beatles's "Eleanor Rigby"

The entrance to the Music Library's reading room

Northwestern's Music Library is among the largest music libraries in the United States and is recognized internationally for its particular commitment to music composed since World War II. The library maintains extensive holdings of works composed since 1945, and since 1971 has collected at least one copy of nearly every new classical score published. The Music Library's entire collection is comprised of more than three hundred thousand volumes of books, scores, sound recordings, journals, and manuscripts, as well as subscriptions to research and audio databases. Its most notable holdings include the John Cage Collection, documenting the life and work of the twentieth century's most revolutionary composer with thousands of letters by and to Cage, photographic scrapbooks, and manuscripts by 274 composers collected by Cage for his book *Notations* (among them, original scribbled lyrics by John Lennon and Paul McCartney for seven Beatles songs, including "Eleanor Rigby" and "Yellow Submarine"). In its General Manuscript Collection, the Music Library holds unique, original manuscripts and correspondence documenting the music and lives of George Crumb, Philip Glass, Karlheinz Stockhausen, Edgard Varèse, Iannis Xenakis, and other prominent composers active since 1945. Additionally, manuscripts of Alban Berg, Francis Poulenc, Maurice Ravel, and other earlier figures represent influences that persist in contemporary music. The Music Library occupies most of Deering Library's main floor and runs continuous exhibits of its holdings in the lobby. A complete list of its resources and services can be found online at www.library.northwestern.edu/music.

Detail from John Cage's manuscript for *Daughters of the Lonesome Isle*

# UNIVERSITY ARCHIVES

Among thousands of photos in the archives is this 1943 image of an 18-year-old Charlton Heston appearing in a student production of *Hedda Gabler*.

The University Archives holds university records of enduring value and other records and papers pertaining to every aspect of Northwestern's history from its founding in 1850. Records range from the handwritten minutes of the May 31, 1850, meeting to found the university to the files of Northwestern presidents and deans through Henry S. Bienen. Especially noteworthy among the personal papers of hundreds of distinguished faculty are those of anthropologist and Africanist Melville J. Herskovits; Pulitzer Prize–winning English professor Ernest Samuels; Winifred Ward, founder of the field of creative dramatics; renowned legal scholar John H. Wigmore; award-winning director Frank Galati; celebrated historians

Clarence L. Ver Steeg and Richard W. Leopold; and physician and public health crusader Isaac Abt. Important records of Northwestern-affiliated organizations include those of the Northwestern University Settlement Association, a pioneering social welfare agency located for more than a century on the near northwest side of Chicago, and the files of dozens of student organizations. Other significant holdings include tens of thousands of biographical files on Northwestern faculty, staff, and alumni; a nearly comprehensive collection of university-generated serial publications, including the *Syllabus* yearbook, the *Daily Northwestern* newspaper, and course catalogs from all of Northwestern's constituent schools; many hundreds of

Archives houses a nineteenth-century telescope used by the Alaskan explorers Robert Kennicott and Henry M. Bannister, whose expedition report helped persuade secretary of state William Seward to purchase Alaska from Russia.

thousands of photographic images; and thousands of motion picture films and audio recordings in many formats. The University Archives reading room is housed in a former seminar classroom on the first level of Deering. More information on University Archives holdings and access, along with quick facts, timelines, and exhibits, is online at www.library.northwestern .edu/archives.

THIS · LIBRARY · WAS
BUILT · BY
NORTHWESTERN
UNIVERSITY
WITH · A · BEQUEST · FROM
CHARLES · DEERING
AND · WITH · GIFTS · FROM
MRS · CHARLES · DEERING
MARION · DEERING
McCORMICK
BARBARA · DEERING
DANIELSON
ROGER · DEERING

JAMES · GAMBLE · ROGERS
ARCHITECT

# LOOKING AHEAD
## A LEGACY FOR RESEARCH LIBRARIANSHIP

There are many layers we bring to the concept of "library": it may mean the books, the building, the favorite interior places, the people we meet in the stacks or on the staff. Now let us extend those images into broader metaphors—the concept of the library as a way of bringing together people and information, in whatever the physical, or now electronic, place of the day. The richness of university libraries is that we expect them to connect us with the entire range of communication formats through history—literally, from clay tablets to the Internet. Deering Library symbolizes this even today. It houses some of the oldest, rarest, and most unusual items in the Northwestern University Library, yet it is also a wireless network node through which those sitting in its reading rooms can link seamlessly to the global digital community of scholars and information resources. If a faculty member needs to compare our clay tablet to one held in a library in Greece, it can be done in a matter of minutes, and without jet lag!

Deering Library is the embodiment of core values that have endured at Northwestern; that is, the centrality of information to the academic endeavor, the need to have ready access to the records of human history and to the results of scientific, artistic, and scholarly productivity. The library, however, extends far beyond these records and beyond even the library walls. It is a set of services, the nexus of many diverse activities that enable these resources to be collected, organized, and used, physically and electronically. The complexity of research libraries is such that these services are constantly shifting, and require extensive external relationships with other libraries, national agencies, vendors, private foundations, and international partners. The history of Northwestern University Library can be traced

SARAH M. PRITCHARD
*Charles Deering McCormick*
*University Librarian*

145

through the growth of these relationships and their impact on resources, services, and technology, from the time Deering Library was built up to the present.

In 1932, Northwestern University was one of the thirty-four founding members of the Association of Research Libraries (ARL), which now represents the 122 largest and most prestigious research libraries in North America. In subsequent years, Northwestern participated directly in numerous projects led by the ARL, the Library of Congress, the Center for Research Libraries, and other institutions that fostered the development of international cataloging standards, purchase agreements for books published overseas, the design of networked computer systems for managing library resources, and the cooperative preservation of those resources through microfilming, shared repositories, and now digital archiving.

It was not long after Deering Library opened that library leaders knew more would be needed, and that the next steps would best be taken in collaboration. In 1940, thirteen university presidents from the Midwest, with support from the Carnegie Foundation, issued a report on the possibility of establishing a cooperative storage and distribution center for little-used books from their collections. Northwestern was again a leader in this group and thus its collections helped create the Midwest Inter-Library Center, now the Center for Research Libraries, to which the Northwestern University Library still contributes. Our students and faculty still benefit by access to this vast array of scholarly resources including historical newspapers, dissertations, scientific literature, government publications, and microfilm from all over the world.

Northwestern University Library's closest "library family" is the eleven other libraries of the institutions that constitute the Committee on Institutional Cooperation (CIC), corresponding approximately to the universities in the Big Ten. Formed in 1956 by the presidents of those universities, the CIC has overseen library initiatives related to interlibrary lending, cross-searching of online library catalogs, shared purchasing, digital repositories, scholarly publishing, and professional training.

Northwestern's contributions to research librarianship, and therefore to the work of students and faculty everywhere, will go down in history thanks to the creation of the library automated system known as NOTIS (Northwestern Online Total Integrated System). Programmed and refined starting in the late 1960s, NOTIS eventually became a successful commercial enterprise independent of the university and was the system of choice for research libraries until the early 1990s. At its peak, NOTIS was used by over 160 libraries, and the profits from the corporate spin-off brought Northwestern University Library a generous endowment that continues to support library technology today. NOTIS may indeed represent the transition from the "Deering" era to that of the Main Library and beyond, as it was envisioned as a crucial component of library expansion and its first segments were timed to be ready with the opening of the Main Library in 1970.

For all libraries, the years since 1970 have been an era of transformation, with the advent of computer technologies that began by radically changing the back-room processing of materials, and have now completely redefined the ways in which information is created, disseminated, and used. Northwestern's innovations in the last decade have paralleled these larger transformations and have built on the cooperative underpinnings of American libraries. New projects to improve the creation and preservation of unique digital collections have been supported by alumni contributions, by the U.S. Institute of Museum and Library Services, and the Andrew W. Mellon Foundation. Most recently Northwestern, with its CIC partners, became a participant in the massive book scanning being undertaken by Google, Inc. The CIC will ultimately establish a shared digital repository for this staggering amount of digitized scholarly work; collections held at Northwestern, including perhaps volumes bought in the earliest days of the library's existence, will be a core component of the repository.

Northwestern University Library has for decades enjoyed a position among the top ten or twelve private university libraries, and among the top thirty for all U.S. academic libraries. Deering Library symbolizes the foundation of this status, in the building of large and substantive collections of scholarly material and archival sources, and in having leadership that contributed nationally to the fabric of research libraries. As we look toward the future, we assess our success in new ways, such as the development of digital collections and the shaping of new services to support faculty research, student learning, publishing, and the stewardship of university digital data. The important traditions of Northwestern University as symbolized by Deering Library will remain vibrant as we work together, on campus and across the globe, to preserve the past and create the future.

# PHOTO CREDITS

The color photographs throughout this book were taken by Peter Kiar. Unless otherwise indicated, all historical photographs and ephemera are held in the Northwestern University Archives; wherever possible, historical photographs have been credited to the original photographer, regardless of the source of the photograph.